Using Diaries for Social Research

INTRODUCING QUALITATIVE METHODS provides a series of volumes which introduce qualitative research to the student and beginning researcher. The approach is interdisciplinary and international. A distinctive feature of these volumes is the helpful student exercises.

One stream of the series provides texts on the key methodologies used in qualitative research. The other stream contains books on qualitative research for different disciplines or occupations. Both streams cover the basic literature in a clear and accessible style, but also cover the 'cutting edge' issues in the area.

SERIES EDITOR
David Silverman (Goldsmiths College)

EDITORIAL BOARD
Michael Bloor (University of Wales, Cardiff)
Barbara Czarniawska-Joerges (University of Gothenburg)
Norman Denzin (University of Illinois, Champaign)
Barry Glassner (University of Southern California)
Jaber Gubrium (University of Missouri)
Anne Murcott (South Bank University)
Jonathan Potter (Loughborough University)

TITLES IN SERIES

Doing Conversation Analysis
Paul ten Have

Using Foucault's Methods
Gavin Kendall and Gary Wickham

The Quality of Qualitative Research
Clive Seale

Qualitative Evaluation
Ian Shaw

Researching Life Stories and Family Histories
Robert L. Miller

Categories in Text and Talk
Georgia Lepper

Focus Groups in Social Research
Michael Bloor, Jane Frankland, Michelle Thomas, Kate Robson

Qualitative Research Through Case Studies
Max Travers

Gender and Qualitative Methods
Helmi Jarviluoma, Pirkko Moisala and Anni Vilkko

Doing Qualitative Health Research
Judith Green and Nicki Thorogood

Methods of critical Discourse Analysis
Ruth Wodak and Michael Meyer

Qualitative Research in Social Work
Ian Shaw and Nick Gould

Qualitative Research in Information Systems
Michael D. Myers and David Avison

Researching the Visual
Michael Emmison and Philip Smith

Qualitative Research in Education
Peter Freebody

Using Documents in Social Research
Lindsay Prior

Doing Research in Cultural Studies
Paula Saukko

Qualitative Research in Sociology: An Introduction
Amir B. Marvasti

Narratives in Social Science
Barbara Czarniawska

Criminological Research: Understanding Qualitative Methods
Lesley Noaks and Emma Wincup

Using Diaries in Social Research
Andy Alaszewski

Using Diaries for Social Research

Andy Alaszewski

SAGE Publications
London ● Thousand Oaks ● New Delhi

First published 2006

Apart from any fair dealing for the purposes of research or private study, or criticism or review, as permitted under the Copyright, Designs and Patents Act, 1988, this publication may be reproduced, stored or transmitted in any form, or by any means, only with the prior permission in writing of the publishers, or in the case of reprographic reproduction, in accordance with the terms of licences issued by the Copyright Licensing Agency. Inquiries concerning reproduction outside those terms should be sent to the publishers.

SAGE Publications Ltd
1 Oliver's Yard
55 City Road
London EC1Y 1SP

SAGE Publications Inc.
2455 Teller Road
Thousand Oaks, California 91320

SAGE Publications India Pvt Ltd
B-42, Panchsheel Enclave
Post Box 4109
New Delhi 110 017

British Library Cataloguing in Publication data

A catalogue record for this book is available from the British Library

ISBN 0 7619 7290 0
ISBN 0 7619 7291 9 (pbk)

Library of Congress Control Number 2005925804

Typeset by C&M Digitals (P) Ltd., Chennai, India
Printed on paper from sustainable resources
Printed in India at Gopsons Paper Ltd, Noida

Contents

Preface

A writer does not always know what he or she knows,
and writing is a way of finding out. (Alan Bennett, 1998,
pp. 539–40)

I first became interested in using diaries for social research in the mid 1990s when
I was commissioned by the English National Board for Nursing Midwifery and
Health Visiting to undertake a study of the ways in which community nurses managed risk in their everyday practice. As part of this research, the research team
wanted to capture and analyse actual clinical decisions and explore their risk implications. Both of the two established approaches, interviewing and observation,
were flawed. Interviews rely on memory, and inviting nurses to recollect specific
decisions was likely to generate generalised and idealised accounts of the ways in
which nurses felt that they should make decisions and manage risk rather than how
they actually did deal with the complexity of specific situations. Observation also
presented problems. It would have intruded into the potentially sensitive relationship between the nurses and their clients and might have distorted the very
processes which we were seeking to capture. We therefore decided to use a less
intrusive approach by inviting nurses to act as self-observers and to record their
observations in diaries (Alaszewski et al., 2000, pp. 81–2).

We then looked for texts that could guide us in this approach. We searched the
obvious social science databases. There was some practical guidance available, for
example Corti (1993), and a number of major studies in our area of interest had
used diaries, for example Robinson (1971) in his study of the process of becoming ill. However the literature was patchy and we found it difficult to identify a
major overview which would provide systematic guidance on the ways in which
diaries could be used for social research. We did identify an article by Zimmerman
and Weider which described a diary-interview approach which they summarised
in the following way:

> Individuals are commissioned by the investigator to maintain ... a record over some speci-
> fied period of time according to a set of instructions ... The technique we described
> emphasizes the role of diaries as an observation log maintained by subjects which can be
> used as a basis for intensive interviewing. (1977, p. 481)

Since this approach seemed to meet our requirements, we decided to use it. However we found it difficult as there was little guidance on the type of instructions to provide, the precise form of the diaries, the ways in which the contents of the diaries were analysed and the ways in which these analyses informed the intensive interviewing.

While the literature on the use of diaries for social research is growing, it does not match that on other commonly used social research methodologies. For example researchers who want to use focus groups as a research method have the choice of a number of excellent texts (Stewart and Shamdasani, 1990; Kreuger, 1994; Kitzinger and Barbour, 1999). Diaries seem to be a neglected source even in areas where one would anticipate they would be a key resource. For example Roberts's (2002) text on biographical research included only one relatively short discussion of diaries.

I really recognised the need for a book on diary research when Bob Heyman invited me to take part in a workshop on qualitative research in primary health care in the North of England. At the conference there were detailed presentations on focus groups and conversational analysis but nothing on diary research apart from my paper. I discussed this with David Silverman and suggested there was room for a book on diary research in the qualitative research series he edited for Sage. He agreed and I offered to submit an outline. I had in mind editing a text that would bring together a range of expertise on the use of diaries, especially in qualitative research. The proposal was accepted with the proviso that it should be a single authored text and should cover the use of diaries in quantitative as well as qualitative research.

It was a major challenge, which I am very pleased that I accepted. In writing the book I found that I knew more than I had anticipated, even if some of this knowledge was only dimly remembered from past academic work and had to be refreshed. However there were still considerable gaps, and writing this book gave me an opportunity to explore areas and forms of research of which I had very little experience or expertise and also made me aware of how flexible and useful diaries are in the research process. This book is designed to contribute to the literature on the use of diaries by providing a text for researchers who are interested in using this methodology. I hope this book will stimulate interest in the use of diaries and stimulate others to write about diary research.

Acknowledgements

I would like to thank David Silverman, editor of the series, for responding positively to my initial suggestions, encouraging me to write a broad overview text and commenting on initial drafts. It has been challenging and it took far longer than anticipated. Partly this reflects my misplaced optimism about the amount of time it would take, but it also reflects some unexpected events in my personal life including a major job change, three house moves and a serious illness. I would like to thank my wife Helen for all her love and support during what was at times a difficult period and for her helpful suggestions for and comments on drafts of this book.

In retrospect my illness did have some positive aspects. It made me concentrate on what I wanted to complete if things went wrong. Getting this book finished became one of my main priorities. The progress of this book was a regular topic of conversation when I met Sharon Beasley and her colleagues at the Maidstone Oncology Centre in Kent and I hope that it justifies the decisions we made.

Writing this book has enabled me to read some wonderful diaries and to find out far more about some fascinating research using diaries. As will be clear I am indebted to some first rate researchers, in particular to Anthony Coxon who commented on an early draft of this book and gave me permission to make use of the first class work published by Project SIGMA. I would like to thank Anthony Coxon and Cassell for permission to quote from his book based on Project SIGMA data, *Between the Sheets* (Coxon, 1996), Louise Corti at the University of Essex and Nigel Gilbert at the University of Surrey for permission to quote from issue 2 of the *Social Research Update* (Corti, 1993) on 'Using diaries in Social Research', Oxford University Press for permission to quote from Alan Bryman's (2001) text on *Social Research Methods* and the management board of *Sociological Research Online* for permission to quote from Heather Elliott's article on 'The use of diaries in sociological research on health experience' (1997). I would also like to thank Jill Manthorpe, Kirstie Coxon and David Wainwright for their comments on early drafts. While I have found all these comments helpful, the final judgement on and responsibility for the published text is mine.

1

The Development and Use of Diaries

The inescapable duty to observe oneself: if someone else is observing me, naturally I have to observe myself too; if none observes me, I have to observe myself all the closer.

Franz Kafka, 7 November 1921

Key aims
- To outline the ways in which diary keeping has developed and key features of diaries.

Key objectives
- To define what a diary is.
- To examine the development and evolution and consider the conditions underpinning the development of diary keeping.
- To consider the publication of diaries and the different types of published diaries.

Definition of diaries

A diary can be defined as a document created by an individual who has maintained a regular, personal and contemporaneous record. Thus the defining characteristics of diaries include:

- *Regularity* A diary is organised around a sequence of regular and dated entries over a period of time during which the diarist keeps or maintains the diary. These entries may be at fixed time intervals such as each day or linked to specific events.
- *Personal* The entries are made by an identifiable individual who controls access to the diary while he or she records it. The diarist may permit others to have access, and failure to destroy the diary indicates a tacit acceptance that others will access the diary.
- *Contemporaneous* The entries are made at the time or close enough to the time when events or activities occurred so that the record is not distorted by problems of recall.
- *A record* The entries record what an individual considers relevant and important and may include events, activities, interactions, impressions and feelings. The record usually takes the form of a time-structured written document, though with the development of technology it can also take the form of an audio or audiovisual recording.

The precise form of diaries varies. The simplest form is the log that contains a record of activities or events without including personal comments on such events. Such personal logs are similar to 'public' journals such as ships' log-books which are regular-entry books whose completion is 'a task, whether officially imposed or self-appointed, performed for its public usefulness' (Fothergill, 1974, p. 16). More complex diaries include not only a record of activities and/or events but also a personal commentary reflecting on roles, activities and relationships and even exploring personal feelings. The diarist may explicitly address different audiences. Elliott (1997, para. 2.2) suggests that diaries whose prime audience is the diarist should be classified as intimate journals, whereas diaries intended for publication and posterity should be classified as a memoir. Such a distinction is difficult to maintain. For example most of the entries which Gladstone, the Victorian politician, made in the diary which he kept for over 71 years were:

> Lists of the persons written to, persons seen, places visited, meetings attended and works read. Once a week or rather more often, Gladstone added a sentence of comment about some individual, event or book, or his own reactions. More rarely he wrote a paragraph, usually of soul-searching. (Beales, 1982, p. 464)

The distinction between intimate journals and memoirs implies that it is possible to clearly discern the motivation of diarists. However it is difficult to make a clear differentiation between private or personal and public. MacFarlane suggests that the term 'diary' can be used for all personal documents which individuals produce about themselves, and uses the term:

> as an all-embracing word [which] includes autobiographies. Often a 'diary' is nothing more than some personal observations scribbled in the margins of an almanack. (1970, p. 4)

The development of diaries

Diaries in their modern form developed in the early modern period in Europe. However there are texts which have some of the features of diaries that predate these by over 500 years.

Japanese 'diaries' and Anglo-Saxon Chronicles

The diary-like documents which predate the development of modern diaries in sixteenth century Europe were produced by literate elites, members of the Japanese Emperor's court and European monks in mediaeval monasteries.

JAPANESE 'DIARIES' By the tenth century courtiers at the Japanese Emperor's court had acquired sufficient expertise in writing to create a vernacular literature. Among the literature which has survived from this period are a number of so-called diaries, including Sei Shonagon's *Pillow Book* (Morris, 1970) and Murasaki Shikibu's diary (Bowring, 1982).

Since the original documents no longer exist, the versions that survive were based on copies which in the case of Sei Shonagon's *Pillow Book* date from the mid thirteenth to the sixteenth centuries (Morris, 1970, p. 12), and it is difficult to be certain about the original content, structure and purpose. Sei Shonagon recorded how in the year 994 the Emperor gave her a gift of paper which she used to record 'odd facts, stories from the past, and all sorts of other things' (1970, p. 11). In contrast, Murasaki's diary appeared to have been written as a record for a third person. Some sections had a letter-like form and there were also references to a third person.

Both texts contained accounts of events that can be clearly dated. In section 82 of the *Pillow Book* (dated to the tenth month of 995) Shonagon records the behaviour of the young Emperor Ichijo on his return from his first independent visit to a shrine dedicated to the god of war, Hachiman:

> When the Emperor returned from his visit to Yawata, he halted his palanquin before reaching the Empress Dowager's gallery and sent a messenger to pay his respects. What could be more magnificent than to see so august a personage as His Majesty seated there in all his glory and honouring his mother in this way? At the sight tears came to my eyes and streamed down my face, ruining my make-up. How ugly I must have looked. (1970, p. 11)

THE SAXON CHRONICLES In Europe writing skills were developed among and monopolised by the clergy, especially scribes in monasteries. In England these scribes used calendars to maintain a record or chronicles. When Saxon monks in preconquest England had to plot the date of Easter, they produced booklets with a line or two for each year and these were filled with 'what might be considered significant events to the institution or locality in which the document was maintained' (Swanton, 2000, p. xi). For example in a surviving set of Easter tables drawn at Canterbury Cathedral covering the years 988 to 1193 a scribe has recorded that in 1066 'Here King Edward passed away', and a later hand added 'and here William came' (2000, p. xiii).

> In its essence the form resembles a diary whose entries were made year by year instead of day by day. It could serve as a repository of the simplest statements of fact, demanding of the compilers no more than a knowledge of writing and of the facts to be recorded, yet at the same time it offered ample scope for a writer who wished to give a detailed account of the events of his day and perhaps even to make his own comments upon them. (Hunter Blair, 1977, p. 352)

These records formed the basis of the Saxon Chronicles which have literary as well as historical interest. For example the victory of the Saxon King Athelstan over the combined Viking, British and Scottish armies was recorded in a poem in the entry for the year 937 in the Parker Chronicle.

> In this year King Athelstan, lord of warriors,
> Ring-giver of men, with his brother prince Edmund,
> Won undying glory with the edges of swords,
> In warfare around *Brunanburh*.
> With their hammered blades, the sons of Edward,
> Clove the shield-wall and hacked the linden bucklers,
> As was instinctive in them, from their ancestry,
> To defend their land, their treasures and their homes,
> In frequent battle against each enemy. (1977, pp. 88–9)

SUMMARY   Both the Japanese 'diaries' and the Saxon Chronicles lacked the full characteristics of modern diaries. Japanese diaries contained both personal accounts and reflections but lacked the clear time structure of modern diaries. While the Saxon Chronicles did form a regular record of contemporary events, they lacked the personal and intimate characteristic of diaries and it is not clear that they were kept contemporaneously.

Box 1.1 Characteristics of early Japanese diaries and Anglo-Saxon Chronicles

	Japanese	*Anglo-Saxon*
Regular, time structured	Possibly	Yes
Personal	Yes but possibly written for third person	No
Contemporaneous Record	Yes but reworked Yes, events and personal reflection	Yes but reworked Yes, events

Development of the diary form in the early modern period

Diaries emerged as a recognisable method of keeping personal records in the early modern period in sixteenth century Europe. In England the young Protestant King, Edward VI, kept a *Chronicle*. It appears that he began the *Chronicle* as an educational and formal exercise for his tutors when he was about 12 years 5 months. Within a year or so it became more personalised and informal in style and he maintained it till shortly before his premature death at the age of 15 (Jordan, 1966, pp. xvii–xviii). The *Chronicle* was a record of events and contained little commentary. For example on 2 May 1550 Edward VI recorded the first execution for heresy in the reign, Joan Bocher, an Anabaptist:

[May, 1550]

2. Joan Bocher, otherwise called Joan of Kent, was burned for holding that Christ was not incarnate of the Virgin Mary, being condemned the year before but kept in hope of conversion; and 30 of April the Bishop of London and the Bishop of Ely were to persuade her. But she withstood them and reviled the preacher that preached at her death. (Jordan, 1966, p. 28)

By the seventeenth century, diary keeping had become an established mechanism for keeping personal records and there was a rapid expansion of the form (MacFarlane, 1970, p. 5). An increasing number of diaries survive from these periods. The most famous were those kept by Samuel Pepys (whose main diary covers the period 1660 to 1669) and John Evelyn (covering his whole lifetime from 1620 to 1706). Diaries were also kept by Robert Hooke, the scientist and architect; John Ray, John Locke and Celia Fiennes, who recorded their travels; Anthony Wood, who recorded university events; John Milward and Anchitel Grey, who recorded parliamentary debates; and Ralph Josselin, who recorded the events of a village from the perspective of a Puritan parson (Latham, 1985, p. xxxv).

The development of diaries during this period was underpinned by technological and socio-economic changes. The technological changes included the widespread development of writing skills in vernacular languages and the production of ready-made almanacs. The socio-economic changes included the fragmentation of Christianity in Western Europe and the rise of Protestantism with its greater emphasis on individualism and the changes associated with the rise of capitalism.

THE TECHNOLOGICAL DEVELOPMENTS UNDERPINNING THE DEVELOPMENT OF DIARIES The main precondition for the development of diary keeping in the seventeenth century was improved access to writing. Prior to the development of modern technologies such as mass production of paper and writing implements such as pens and pencils, writing was a complex and expensive technology restricted to an elite who were specially selected and trained. The difference between the language used for writing and the vernacular language used for everyday communication created an additional barrier to wider access to writing. In mediaeval Western Europe, the written language used by the Church and for international contact was Latin. Reading and writing were taught in schools associated with monasteries and cathedrals, some of which developed into universities (Janson, 2002, p. 168). The changes associated with the Reformation and the emergence of Protestantism in Northern Europe in the sixteenth century had a major impact on literacy. These new churches emphasised the importance of lay access to religious knowledge so that:

> the clergy should preach the Christian faith in the languages spoken by the people, and that the central texts should be available in those languages. (2002, p. 168)

This stimulated a related technological development, printing, which was used to produce bibles and other religious texts in vernacular languages. This increased access to written texts in turn increased the opportunity and incentive to learn to read and write. Thus by the end of the sixteenth century writing was becoming an increasingly accessible skill.

An early by-product of the new printing technology was the publication of almanacs, annual calendars of events, which had spaces for individual annotation and facilitated diary keeping (Latham, 1985, p. xxxv). Such early diaries were often extensions of household accounts but also included observations of events or happenings that attracted the diarist's interest or curiosity. There was awareness that such records could be used as a method of systematic observation and learning. Francis Bacon in his *Essayes* emphasised the educational value of travel for young men and the role which a diary could play in maximising the learning opportunities of such travel by providing a systematic record of the diarist's observations. Bacon's *Essayes* evolved over a 30-year period in the early seventeenth century (1597–1625) and were intended to be a guide or 'conduct book' for civil or public business (Kiernan, 1985b, pp. xix–xx):

> *Traivaile*, in the younger Sort, is a Part of Education; In the Elder, a Part of Experience … It is a strange Thing, that in Sea voyages, where there is nothing to be seene, but Sky and Sea, Men should make Diaries; But in *Land-Travaile*, wherein so much is to be observed, for the most part they omit it; As if Chance, were fitter to be registred, than Observation. Let Diaries, therefore, be brought into use. (italics in the original: Kiernan, 1985a, p. 56)

John Evelyn followed Bacon's advice and his diary was designed as a complete record of his life and the events he observed. His full *Kalendarium, My Journal &c* amounts to over half a million words. It covers his whole life from his birth on 30 October 1620 until 3 February 1706, just a few weeks before his death on 27 February (de la Bédoyère, 1994, p. 15). Evelyn's diary records contemporary events in England. In 1688 he records the invasion of William of Orange and the plight of James II:

November 8   I went to Lond: heard the newes of the Princes of Oranges being landed at Tor-bay, with a fleete of neere 700 saile, so dreadfull a sight passing through the Channell with so favorable a Wind, as our Navy could by no meanes intercept or molest them: This put the King & Court into greate Consternation, now employed in forming an Army to incounter their farther progresse. (1994, p. 357)

While Evelyn provided an account of events, his personality and opinions shine through.

THE SOCIO-ECONOMIC DEVELOPMENTS UNDERPINNING THE DEVELOPMENT OF DIARIES   The development and popularity of diary keeping can also be linked to the socio-economic changes associated with the emergence of modern individualism based on the development of capitalism and Protestantism which, as Weber (1976) argued, were linked.

The evolution of individual identity is perhaps most evident in the artistic sphere in the late fifteenth century when artists began to challenge the control that patrons exerted over their work and claimed ownership over the intellectual content of their creativity. These moves culminated in the development of individual control of intellectual property in modern copyright legislation (Carter-Ruck et al., 1965, pp. 28–9). Albrecht Dürer, a North European artist, played an important role in developments. He maximised the commercial value of his work by using the newly developed printing technology to create saleable reproductions. To differentiate his work from others he created a distinctive personal identifier for each work. He developed his initials into a clearly definable mark, perhaps the first example of a commercial logo.

In 1520 and 1521 Dürer visited the Netherlands, mainly on a business trip. He wanted the new Holy Roman Emperor Charles to confirm his imperial pension, and while he was in Antwerp he wanted to sell his collections of woodcuts and engravings (Goris and Marlier, 1970, p. 8). During his visits, Dürer kept a diary. It was primarily a record of his receipts and expenses including his gambling (1970, p. 8). However he also recorded his reaction to the 'men, artists, places, monuments and works of art he encountered in the Netherlands' (1970, p. 9) including his reaction to the news that Martin Luther had been taken prisoner and his life threatened:

On Friday before Whitsunday in the year 1521, came tidings to me at Antwerp that Martin Luther had been so treacherously taken prisoner; for he trusted Emperor Charles, who had granted him his herald and imperial safe-conduct. But as soon as the herald had conveyed him to an unfriendly place near Eisenach he rode away, saying he no longer needed him. Straightway there appeared ten knights and they treacherously carried off the pious man, betrayed into their hands, a man enlightened by the Holy Ghost, a follower of the true Christian faith. And whether he yet lives I know not, or whether they have put him to death; if so, he has suffered for the truth of Christ and because he rebuked the unchristian Papacy, which strives with its heavy load of laws against the redemption of Christ. (1970, p. 90)

Protestantism, especially the development of North European Puritan sects, played a key role in the development of diaries. It stimulated the development of vernacular writing, and provided an incentive for using diaries to record and reflect upon personal actions and activities. Puritans emphasised the importance of the direct relationship between the individual and God. Pollock noted that Puritans had an 'inexorable drive to put their thoughts to paper as a means of cultivating the holy life by techniques of self-examination and self-revelation' (1983, p. 70). Documents such as diaries formed an important part of this self-examination:

> The diary-keeping that is so significant a symptom of the new type of character may be viewed as a kind of inner time-and-motion study by which the individual records and judges his output day by day. It is evidence of the separation between the behaving and scrutinizing self. (Reisman, cited in MacFarlane, 1970, p. 5)

Tomalin identified the influence of religious factors when discussing the reasons why Samuel Pepys kept a diary:

> At Cambridge puritan divines … recommended Christian diary-keeping as a valuable exercise, a form of moral accounting that encouraged the individual to watch and discipline himself. John Beadle's *The Journal or Diary of a Thankful Christian*, published in 1656, also approved the keeping of a diary and suggested it should include public events and private experience. (2002, p. 81)

Pepys's diary reflected his Puritan education. He used his diary to confess his sins. He used a shorthand system, which he probably learned as an undergraduate at the University of Cambridge (Latham, 1985, p. xiv). This protection meant that Pepys felt confident enough to use his diary to candidly examine his own motives, emotions and lusts. For example on 24 September 1663 he recorded an illicit liaison with a Mrs Lane in Deptford, making the following entry in this diary:

> After being tired of her [Mrs Lane's] company, I landed her at Whitehall and so home and at my office writing letters, till 12 at night almost; and then home to supper and bed and there find my poor wife hard at work, which grieved my heart to see that I should abuse so good a wretch, and that it is just with God to make her bad to me for my wronging of her; but I do resolve never to do the like again. So to bed. (Latham, 1985, p. 311)

Pepys was a self-made man who acquired his wealth and status, at least in part, through his own skill and judgement. Pepys's public career was closely linked to the Restoration monarchy, as is his diary. He started his diary in 1660 when he accompanied his patron Lord Sandwich to the Continent to escort the restored monarch, Charles II, back to England, and stopped in 1669 following his unfounded fear that writing a diary was making him blind. While Pepys's diary is 'primarily a personal journal, [it] was designed also as a chronicle of public affairs' (Latham and Matthews, 1970a, p. cxv). He recorded his own role in such affairs and also used this record as a resource to protect himself from inevitable political attack (Latham, 1985, p. xxxiii) and to publicly claim credit for his role in state affairs. While his diary remained private in his lifetime, he used it when defending his actions before Parliament and in preparing his *Memoires Relating to the State of the Royal Navy* which were published in 1690 and outlined his role in the development of the Navy.

Box 1.2 The preconditions for the development of diaries in the early modern period

Technology

- Written version of the vernacular language
- Paper preferably bound in books or almanacs
- Writing equipment – ink, pens/brushes

Skills

- Schools providing training in writing
- Individuals with the skills, equipment, time and opportunity to keep a private record

Motivation

- Perceived benefits (spiritual/personal, financial, political, social) of keeping a private record
- Means of ensuring the diary is not used to discredit the diary keeper, i.e. personal privacy and security

---

Development of the diary form

Diary keeping in sixteenth and seventeenth century England developed in a very distinctive social and religious environment that influenced both the motivations for keeping diaries and the forms of diaries. By the nineteenth century diary keeping had become a 'conventional habit among persons of culture' (Fothergill, 1974, p. 34):

> Faithfully and earnestly penned by hosts of respectable people – ladies and travellers, intellectuals and politicians, clergymen and soldiers, and the Queen – these diaries contain an enormously detailed picture of life within the Victorian social fabric, and reflect contemporary attitudes and values with great fidelity. (1974, p. 34)

These diaries exhibited growing literary self-consciousness as diarists became increasingly aware of the possibility of publication. For example Barbellion

(1919) maintained a diary from 1903 which appears to end with a note on 31 December 1917 recording the diarist's death. Barbellion described his struggle to develop a career as a biologist despite ill-health. However, as Fothergill noted, Barbellion actually prepared the diary for publication before his death in 1919 and intended it be 'an epoch-making work of fearless self-revelation' (1974, p. 35).

This increased self-consciousness is related to surveillance of the self both by the diarist and by others. The prime motivation of the self-surveillance in early diaries is religious; however, with the secularisation of society and the development of psychoanalytical theory, diaries can be used to understand and manage the self. For example Graham Greene, the twentieth century novelist, following his psychoanalysis as a young man recorded his dreams in his diary to monitor his unconscious mind. Anaïs Nin, a novelist who also trained as a psychoanalyst, kept a diary which has been described as a 'record of a modern woman writer's journey of self-discovery' (Stuhlmann, 1974, rear cover). In her entry for the month of April 1935 she described her decision to choose the role and identity of a novelist rather than a psychoanalyst:

> There was a meeting of psychoanalysts, and there were seven of us in the train going to Long Beach ... It was that day, at a dinner, with a tag on my shoulder, that I discovered I did not belong to the world of psychoanalysis. My game was always exposed. At the door there is always a ticket collector asking: 'Is it real? Are you real? Are you a psychoanalyst?' They always know I am a fraud. They do not take me in ... I was not a scientist. I was seeking a form of life which was continuous like a symphony. The key word was the sea ... I could not hear the discussion. I was listening for the sea's roar and pulse. It was that day I realized that I was a writer, and only a writer, a writer and not a psychoanalyst. (1974, pp. 45–6)

The role of the diary as a mechanism for surveillance is evident in twentieth century diary keeping, especially in the 'reflective journal'. In human services reflective journals have become one way of monitoring and enhancing the personal development and performance of professionals, especially in initial training programmes. As Bain and his colleagues (1999, p. 52) have noted journal writing is a recognised way of teaching in counselling, psychology, nursing, management, leadership and teaching. Wellard and Bethune (1996, p. 1077) suggested that reflective journal writing has become the road to the Holy Grail in nurse education. Riley-Doucet and Wilson (1997) gave a description of reflective journals used in their nurse education programme and made it clear that such journals have all the defining characteristics of diaries:

> All students are asked to keep a journal of their clinical experiences with daily entries throughout the academic semester. The journal is the private property of the student. The student is not required to show the journal to the nursing educator, although this is certainly offered as a means of gaining feedback from the educator regarding their acquisition of critical thinking skills. It is essential that the student is given the option of keeping

their journal private and confidential, so that the journal becomes a safe place for self-disclosure and self-reflection. (1997, p. 965)

While Riley-Doucet and Wilson stressed the self-surveillance role of reflective journals, it is clear from their accounts that such journals were incorporated into broader surveillance. The journals not only formed part of peer group discussion but were also used in the formal evaluation process (1997, p. 965), creating a power imbalance between educator and trainee professional (Wellard and Bethune, 1996). While the use of diaries as a mechanism of surveillance may be seen as relatively benign in this context, in totalitarian states it is more sinister. Sun Yushun, who grew up in Mao's China, described how she kept a diary which recorded her use of Mao's *Little Red Book* and how she read out sections of her diary in class. For example when she was 10 she read out the following entry:

> Our great leader, teacher and helmsman Chairman Mao said that unity was paramount: without it, there would have been no victory for the Communist Party. But I fought with my brother today. If I could not even unite with him, how could I do so with all the people in the motherland? If people do not unite, how are we going to realise the goal of communism, paradise on earth? Must read more of Chairman Mao's works, listen to him more attentively, and be his good child. (Yushun, 2003, p. 6)

In the twentieth century new forms of technology created new opportunities for diary keeping. For example relatively inexpensive audio and video recorders have provided the opportunity for audio and video diaries. Ellen MacArthur, during her record-breaking solo round-the-world sailing voyage, recorded audio and video reports which were posted on a website (MacArthur, 2005). The proliferation of technology for recording and communicating sound and image has created the opportunity for mixed media diaries. Lynn Redgrave, a British actress, when she was diagnosed as having breast cancer, decided to collaborate with her daughter on a project to record her treatment and recovery. Lynn kept a written record and her daughter, Annabel Clark, a photographic record which they used to produce a journal combining visual images and text, extracts from which were published in a British weekend colour supplement (Redgrave and Clark, 2004). In the extract the final photograph of Lynn Redgrave after her operation is accompanied by the following text describing why she had decided not to have breast reconstruction:

Monday, August 11 [2003]

> I had this vision of altering oneself – cutting oneself, not worthy, not beautiful unless … and I'm thinking, as I sit on my porch with candles and wine – no. My lesson to learn through my long-ago eating disorder, through my cancer, my acting, my life, my loss of youth, my lesson is that the essential core of me is right here – unadorned, single breasted – that's a way to look at it. (2004, p. 20)

The World Wide Web has created a major opportunity for diary keeping. Individuals can record their everyday life and post it on the web. There is a number of websites providing access to 'diaper diaries' recording the experience of bringing up babies (Brown, 2005; Armstrong, 2005) and 'blogs' or weblogs. McClellan (2005) described the University of Warwick Blog project which encouraged students to write online journals or weblogs; the website (http://blogs.warwick.ac.uk) hosted over 3,000 weblogs.

COMMENT   While the early diarists established many of the features and conventions of diary writing, the development of the form reflects changing social context. Through the form and context of each diary reflects the specific purpose and motivation of its diarist, it is possible to identify trends, especially the development of increased literary self-awareness reflecting greater awareness of the opportunities for publication. In this context the distinction between a diary and an autobiography is blurred. As diaries are increasingly published or 'made public', so it is possible to identify a surveillance function. The development of an interest in and concern with the development of the self and personal identity that is evident in psychoanalysis can also be found in diaries. They can be used as a mechanism for self-surveillance and for external surveillance and shaping of the developing person as in reflective journal and reflective practice. In modern society an individual's social standing and identity are relatively flexible and fluid and need to be created and protected. Diaries provide one way of creating and protecting such standing and identity.

Box 1.3 Development of the diary form

Technology

- Development of new forms of recording technology, including photography, audio and video recording
- Development of new forms of communication including radio, television and the internet

Access to resources

- In most developed countries, high levels of literacy and relatively low cost of traditional diaries and increasing access to audio and video recording equipment
- Increased personal security
- Increased openness of communication media such as newspapers and internet

Pressures and motivation

- External scrutiny and surveillance
- Increased awareness of self and need to develop and account for self

Publication: diaries and autobiography

While the diary as an individual mechanism for recording and commenting on events and activities became popular in the seventeenth century, public access to diaries did not develop until the nineteenth century when publishers recognised a market for such personal records. For example William Upcott discovered Evelyn's diary during a social call to the widow of the diarist's great-great-grandson and subsequently published it in 1818 (de la Bédoyère, 1994, p. 16). This stimulated moves to transcribe and publish Pepys's diary and the first edited version was published in 1825 (Latham and Matthews, 1970b, pp. lxxiv–lxxxiii). The process of publication can change the status of a diary from a private personal record to a publicly available document or biography. In this section I will explore some types of published diaries.

The diary as a record of facts

The expansion of European power in the sixteenth century was linked to increased knowledge and control of both the physical and the social world. It was associated with both factual and fictional accounts of voyages of discovery (Howell, 2002). By the eighteenth and nineteenth centuries public interest in the major scientific discoveries created a market for accounts of such voyages. Captain James Cook's and Charles Darwin's journals provided accounts of their voyages of discovery.

Captain Cook was commissioned to undertake three voyages to the Pacific between 1768 and 1780. The stated aim of the first voyage was to undertake observations of the transit of Venus on 3 June 1769 on behalf of the Royal Society, an important English association of scientists, so that an accurate assessment could be made of the distance from the earth to the sun. Cook also had secret instructions from the British Admiralty to look for and explore the lands that lay to the south of the observation point (Beaglehole, 1988a, pp. cix–cxi and cclxxii). Not only did Cook maintain a journal of all three voyages but other members of his crew also kept diaries. One incident in the journals has attracted particular interest: Cook's death in Hawaii on Sunday 14 February 1779. It seems to epitomise the conflict and mutual misunderstanding between expanding European imperialism and the traditional cultures which it affected. Samwell's journal included the following entry, a graphic account of Cook's death:

> Captain Cook was now the only Man on the Rock, he was seen walking down towards the Pinnace, holding his left hand against the Back of his head to guard it from the Stones & carrying his Musket under the other Arm. An Indian came running behind him, stopping once or twice as he advanced, as if he was afraid that he should turn round, then taking him unaware he sprung to him, knocked him on the back of his head with a large Club taken out of a fence, & instantly fled with the greatest precipitation; the blow made Captain Cook stagger two or three paces, he then fell on his hand & one knee & dropped his Musket, as he was rising another Indian came running to him & before he could ·

recover himself from the Fall drew out an iron Dagger he concealed under his feathered Cloak & struck it with all his force into the back of his Neck, which made Capt. Cook tumble into the Water in a kind of a bite by the side of the rock where the water is about knee deep; here he was followed by a croud of people who endeavoured to keep him under water, but struggling very strong with them he got his head up & looking towards the Pinnace which was not above a boat hook's Length from him waved his hands to them for Assistance, which it seems it was not in their Power to give. The Indians got him under water again but he disengaged himself & got his head up once more & not being able to swim he endeavoured to scramble on the Rock, when a fellow gave him a blow on the head with a large Club and he was seen alive no more. They now kept him under water, one man sat on his Shoulders & beat his head with a stone while others beat him with Clubs & Stones, they then hauled him up dead where they stuck him with their Daggers, dashed his head against the rock and beat him with Clubs and Stones, taking a Savage pleasure in using every barbarity to the dead body. (Beaglehole, 1988b, p. 1198)

Cook's mapping of the Pacific was continued by various ships of the British Navy including HMS *Beagle* which was commissioned to complete a survey of Patagonia and Tierra del Fuego. The *Beagle* set sail in 1826 to survey the shores of Chile, Peru and some islands in the Pacific including the Galapagos Islands. The expedition included a 'scientific person', Charles Darwin. In 1845 Darwin published 'in the form of a Journal, a history of our voyage, and a sketch of those observations in Natural History and Geology, which I think will possess some interest to the general reader' (1888, p. v). The journal anticipated Darwin's *The Origin of Species by Means of Natural Selection* (1951) in which he fully and explicitly expounded his theory of evolution. In his entry for 8 October 1835 Darwin wrote an extended commentary on the natural history of the Galapagos and commented on the ways in which one bird species had evolved on the islands to fill different ecological niches:

> Seeing this gradation and diversity of structure in one small, intimately related group of birds, one might really fancy that from an original paucity of birds in this archipelago, *one species had been taken and modified for different ends.* (italics added: 1888, p. 380)

Such scientific journals purported to record facts whose significance could be subsequently evaluated. In the case of Cook's voyage the value of the facts was both strategic and scientific. All the men keeping diaries aboard had to hand in their diaries to the captain at the end of the voyage and were enjoined to secrecy over their discoveries (Beaglehole, 1988b, p. 1295).

The memoir: creating a record for posterity

Monarchs, statesmen and politicians like to construct monuments which highlight their achievements. While Roman Emperors built monuments – for example, the Emperor Trajan built a column highlighting his triumphs – in contemporary society such monuments often take the form of written accounts or memoirs. Politicians have used diaries to provide immediacy and authenticity to such accounts.

In the United Kingdom, the first politician known to keep a diary with a view to publication was Hugh Dalton, a senior minister in the 1945–51 Labour government. Pimlott (2002) has suggested that Dalton wrote his diary for personal enjoyment rather than for financial rewards. Pimlott notes the ways in which Dalton recorded and commented on his colleagues in the British Labour Party:

> When his diaries were published in 1952, Herbert Morrison happened to be dining with Jim Callaghan and his wife, and found a copy in the loo. 'I didn't know the bugger kept a diary like that,' growled the former foreign secretary as he emerged. Callaghan promptly reported the remark to his friend Dalton – who gleefully recorded it in his still-continuing diary. (2002, p. 2)

The 1960s Labour Cabinet included three diarists, Tony Benn, Barbara Castle and Richard Crossman. Crossman died in 1974 and the second and third volumes of his diaries were published posthumously; Janet Morgan had to complete the editorial work. Crossman dictated his diary while the 'memory was still hot' and then prepared the published version (Morgan, 1977, p. 9) in which he recorded events and his feelings about them. The first entry in this diary recorded his first visit to his new ministry:

Monday, April 22nd [1968]

> I made my first visit to the collection of huge modern glass blocks that was custom-built for the Ministry of Health at the Elephant and Castle. It is on a ghastly site and Kenneth Robinson [previous minister] told me they chose it for its cheapness. It cost only half as much as normal sites for government buildings but a great deal of the money they saved is now being spent on air-conditioning and double-glazing because the building stands right on top of an under-ground railway which makes the most dreadful din. It's also appallingly inconvenient … It was hoped that one effect of planking [sic] the building down there would be to improve the area and attract other government buildings. It hasn't happened and the Ministry stands isolated and terrible. (Crossman, 1977, p. 17)

Since the memoir-diary form was first used in the 1940s, it has become increasingly popular and profitable. Individual politicians supported by editors can rapidly produce accounts of and commentaries on events and cast themselves as neutral independent observers who are giving readers a privileged access to decisions or events as they happen.

Bearing witness: the diary as a personal testimony of suffering

While public figures and celebrities with a media profile use diaries to 'record' their role and response to public and private affairs, diaries can be used by individuals to record or even bear witness to events, especially those involving personal or collective suffering. The Second World War and the Holocaust involved intensive suffering and Anne Frank's diary has become particularly well known. Anne was a young Jewish girl who lived in Amsterdam. She started her first diary on 12 June 1942 and recorded events of her everyday life, for example her opinions of other pupils in her class at her Jewish school. However when her father was 'called up' on 8 July 1942 by the German authorities, a euphemism for being sent to the concentration camps, she and her family went into hiding (A. Frank, 1997, p. 19) and her diaries recorded the pressures of her exceptional life in hiding. As her diary moved towards its close, the family were taken into custody by the Nazi authorities on 4 August 1944 and sent to concentration camps where Anne died in a typhoid epidemic (O. Frank, 1997b, pp. 338–9). Just before her arrest, Anne wrote to her fictional friend in her diary commenting poignantly on her situation (A. Frank, 1997, p. 330):

SATURDAY 15 JULY 1944

Dearest Kitty,

It's utterly impossible for me to build my life on a foundation of chaos, suffering and death. I see the world being slowly transformed into a wilderness, I hear the approaching thunder that, one day, will destroy us too, I feel the suffering of millions. And yet, when I look up at the sky, I somehow feel that everything will change for the better, that this cruelty too will end, that peace and tranquillity will return once more. In the meantime, I must hold on to my ideals. Perhaps the day will come when I'll be able to realize them!

Yours, Anne M. Frank

Many recent diaries bear witness to more personal events and experiences such as the impact of illness. Robert McCrum, a journalist, experienced a stroke when he was 42 and both he and his wife kept diaries recording their experiences. He used these diaries to produce an account of the consequences of his stroke. In his book McCrum provided graphic examples of the practical problems he encountered when trying to reconstruct his life and the support he received from his wife. Shortly after his stroke, which happened on the night of 28–29 July 1995, McCrum recorded in his diary some of his practical difficulties and the support he was receiving from his wife:

[Monday 7 August 1995]

I shave sitting in the bath, looking at my reflection in the bath taps. I have not seen my face in a mirror since I fell ill, and I'm frightened at what I might find. (In fact, apart from a slightly drooping left side to my face and an expression of great sadness, I find that I am not a freak.) Afterwards I clean my teeth one-handed with considerable difficulty (*it's surprisingly hard to unscrew a tube of toothpaste one-handed*) and get given fresh clothes. Then I am wheeled back to my room. Now I am sitting in a chair with my headache and Sarah is on the phone. Sarah seems to have understood my condition very well, and is tremendously organised. She is being quite amazing. (McCrum, 1998, p. 75, emphasis added)

McCrum provided extracts from his wife's diary which indicated that while she was supporting and reassuring him, the stroke was having a major impact on her life and she was experiencing her own anxiety and fear:

SARAH'S DIARY: SUNDAY 6 AUGUST

I feel so very sad and scared. R. making progress but he is so depressed and so unable to try – the smallest thing tires him out – it's as if he doesn't care. I worry, I worry, that this has changed him, that he is not the same man. We went into the Square, him in a wheel-chair, today, and my heart just about broke. What are we going to do? I don't know who he is, who I am, what we've gotten ourselves into. I feel that I have no one in the world to lean on, no one to help me. What if it never gets any better? What will I do then? If I keep his spirits up, I wonder, will I actually be able to do something for him, or is it just hopeless? I feel bone tired and not up to it, and so very, very frightened. (1998, p. 75)

Diaries such as Anne Frank's and Robert and Sarah McCrum's bear witness to suffering. The diarists, or in the case of Anne Frank, her father Otto, were willing to publish these diaries and make their contents public to provide insight into and understanding of the personal consequences of an event such as the Holocaust.

The artistic journal

Given the skills which writers display in producing fiction, it is hardly surpris-ing that they should use these skills in recording and commenting on their everyday life and the ways in which they produce their fiction. Some writers have seen their diaries as a purely personal record and have ensured their destruction. Philip Larkin, the English poet, wrote over 30 volumes of his diary which were shredded shortly after his death (Motion, 1993, p. 522). However such destruction appears to be the exception and writers' diaries form a substantial body of literature in their own right.

Virginia Woolf, a major twentieth century writer, kept a diary for most of her life and the publication of her diaries provided a record of her struggles to write. The final published volume of her diary covered the last five years of her life and started with her struggles to complete one of her major works, *The Years*, and ended four days before she drowned herself on 28 March 1941. In her diary Virginia Woolf documented her continued struggles against depres-sion and her feeling about the war. For example on Sunday 26 January 1941 she outlined how she responded to the rejection of a story by a magazine and the political situation:

This trough of despair shall not, I swear, engulf me … Sleep & slackness; musing; reading; cooking; cycling; oh & a good hard rather rocky book – viz: Herbert Fisher. This is my prescription ... There's a lull in the war. 6 nights without raids. But Garvin says the greatest struggle is about to come – say in 3 weeks – & every man, woman dog cat even weevil must girt their arms, their faith – & so on.

It's the cold hour, this, before the lights go up. A few snowdrops in the garden. Yes, I was thinking: we live without future. Thats whats queer, with our noses pressed to a closed door. Now to write, with a new nib, to Enid Jones. (Olivier Bell, 1984, p. 17)

The Czech writer Franz Kafka also kept a diary. This was very much a sketchbook in which he recorded his thoughts and ideas. Indeed the link between his diary and his other fictional work is so strong that his diaries are included as part of a compendium of his work. Like Virginia Woolf, Kafka recorded his personal struggles. In his case these included tensions over his Jewish identity and the challenges to his mental wellbeing (Kafka, 1976, p. 849).

Artists' diaries can be treated both as a record of the creative process and as a product of the creative process having the same status as their other writing. It is therefore hardly surprising that there should be blurring between fact and fiction, with some writers using the diary as a fictional form. As the introduction to Kafka's collected work noted: 'In Kafka the autobiographical and the fictional are so intertwined that it is futile to try to unravel them' (1976, p. xi).

The diary as fiction

The narrative structure of the diary provides a 'natural' form which can be used for narrator-centred fiction and was extensively exploited by Daniel Defoe in the early seventeenth century. Three of his major works exploited the form: *A Journal of the Plague Year* (1722) (Backsheider, 1992), *Memoirs of a Cavalier* (1720) (Boulton, 1991) and *Robinson Crusoe* (1719) (Shinagel, 1994). The original title page of each work clearly signals Defoe's narrative form, for example:

A JOURNAL OF THE **Plague Year:** Being Observations or Memorials, Of the most remarkable OCCURRENCES, As well PUBLICK *as* PRIVATE, Which happened in LONDON During the last GREAT VISITATION In 1665. Written by a CITIZEN who continued all the while in *London*. Never made publick before. (Backsheider, 1992, p. 3)

Gogol, a Russian writer, also used the form in his *Diary of a Madman* first published in 1834. In the diary Gogol chronicled the increasing delusions of his diarist and especially his diarist's conviction that he was the King of Spain. The 'diarist' exhibited his madness and his 'rational' irrationality in the following entry:

No date: The day didn't have one

I walked incognito down Nevsky Avenue [St Petersburg]. His Imperial Majesty drove past. Every single person doffed his hat, and I followed suit. However, I didn't let out that I was the King of Spain. I considered it improper to reveal my true identity right there in the middle of the crowd, because according to etiquette, I ought first to be presented at court. So far, the only thing that had stopped me was not having any royal clothes. If only I could get hold of a cloak. (Gogol, 1972, p. 36)

Although Defoe's and Gogol's writing are clearly fictional, commentators linked them to historical research. For example a critical edition of Defoe's *A Journal of the Plague Year* included other plague narratives as well as Foucault's sociological analysis of surveillance and the 'panopticon' as a response to plague (Backsheider, 1992, pp. 244–50). In an article in the *British Medical Journal*, Altschuler argued that Gogol's fictional work is 'one of the oldest and most complete descriptions of schizophrenia' (2001, p. 1475).

Box 1.4 Some forms of published diaries

Diary as scientific 'record'

- Author absent or presents self as neutral observer
- Narrative of discovery in which the strange and unfamiliar are recorded
- Reader offered experience and insight

Diary as memoire

- Author is an 'important' person who claims privileged access to key events and decisions
- Narrative based on author's role and contribution to events and decisions
- Reader offered opportunity to see events 'through the eyes' of the author

Diary bearing witness

- Author presents self as 'ordinary person' experiencing or surviving extraordinary events
- Narrative of suffering and survival
- Reader offered access and insight into 'how it feels'

Literary diary

- Author claims status as a 'writer'
- Narrative of author's struggle to create
- Reader offered insight into the creative process as well as a product of that process

Fictional diary

- Fictional narrator who claims status of an independent often scientific observer
- Narrative of discovery and revelation
- Reader offered insight through fictional world

Comment

Publication changes the status and nature of diaries. The 'original diary' has to be prepared for publication. Anne Frank rewrote her diary in response to a radio broadcast from Gerrit Bolkestein, a member of the Dutch government in exile who asked for letters and diaries so that he could collect eyewitness accounts of the suffering imposed on the Netherlands by the Nazi regime (O. Frank, 1997a, pp. v–viii) and her father edited the published version. Unpublished and published diaries share features in common, especially the diarist's/author's use of a time framework to create a record and narrative structure. However they differ in terms of their readership: the readership of unpublished diaries is restricted to those who have access, in the first instance the diarist, whereas published diaries are targeted to a wider audience.

Summary and comment

The development of diary keeping was a product of technical changes which increased access to the resources needed to write diaries, and the social and religious changes that provided the stimulus and motivation for maintaining a personal record. With the reduced cost of publication, an increasing number of diaries have been published and made accessible to the public. It is possible to identify within these diaries a diversity of form and function ranging from 'factual' accounts of discoveries to fictional accounts of insanity. While the purpose and structure of diaries vary they provide a rich source of data for social researchers, and in the next chapter we will consider how diaries can and have been used in research.

KEY POINTS

Diary keeping

- Diary keeping is a recognised form of social activity.
- Diary keeping can only develop and flourish when certain conditions are met: there is a written vernacular language; there are lay groups within society who have the skills and resources to use this written language as a medium for keeping a personal record; and the incentives for these groups to keep a diary outweigh the risks.
- It is possible to recognise diary-like documents in some premodern societies but diary keeping in its modern form developed in Europe in the early modern period.
- While religious developments were an initial stimulus to diary keeping, diaries in contemporary society are kept for a variety of reasons and take a variety of forms.

Publication

- Given the interest in and market for diaries, there is now a substantial number of published diaries.

- Published diaries vary in form and structure from factual/scientific journals to fictional diaries.
- It is possible to identify distinctive conventions in the different forms, related to the role of the narrator, the nature of the narrative and the role of the reader.

EXERCISE

The best way of developing an understanding of the ways in which diaries have developed and the conventions that underpin diary writing is to read some diaries. This should not be a great chore as most published diaries are both interesting and in some cases beautifully written. While most of the more popular diaries are in print, often in abbreviated forms, and can be purchased, they are also widely available in libraries. So I suggest that you access one of the diaries from each of lists A, B and C. Read the introduction to each diary and at least 10 pages of the main diary and then consider the issues raised.

Diaries which can be used in the exercise

The diaries are grouped into three categories: historic, contemporary and fictional.

List A: historic diaries

Japanese
Bowring, R. (1982) *Murasaki Shikubu: Her Diary and Poetic Memoir*, trans. and ed. R. Bowring, Princeton University Press, Princeton, NJ.
Morris, I. (ed.) (1970) *The Pillow Book of Sei Shonagon*, trans. and ed. Ivan Morris, Penguin, Harmondsworth.

Early modern
de la Bédoyère (ed.) (1994) *The Diary of John Evelyn*, Headstart History, Bangor.
Goris, J.-A. and Marlier, G. (1970) *Albrecht Dürer: Diary of his Journey to the Netherlands 1520–1521*, intro. J.-A. Goris and G. Marlier, Lund Humphries, London.
Jordan, W.K. (ed.) (1966) *The Chronicle and Political Papers of King Edward VI*, Allen and Unwin, London.
Latham, R. (ed.) (1985) *The Shorter Pepys,* selected and ed. R. Latham, Bell and Hyman, London.

Voyages
Beaglehole, J.C. (1988) *The Journals of Captain James Cook on his Voyages of Discovery: the Voyage of the Endeavour, 1768–1771, Part One*, Kraus Reprint, Millwood, NY.

(Continued)

(Continued)

Darwin, C. (1888) *A Naturalist's Voyage: Journal of Researches into the Natural History and Geology of the Countries Visited during the Voyage of H.M.S. 'Beagle' round the World*, Murray, London.

Political
Foote, M.R.D. (1968) *The Gladstone Diaries, vol. 1 (1825–1832)*, Clarendon, Oxford.
Foote, M.R.D. (1968) *The Gladstone Diaries, vol. 2 (1833–1839)*, Clarendon, Oxford.
Helps, A. (1868) *Leaves from the Journal of Our Life in the Highlands: Victoria, Queen of England*, Smith, Elder, London.

Social
Hudson, D. (ed.) (1972) *Munby, Man of Two Worlds: the Life and Diaries of Arthur J. Munby 1828–1910*, Murray, London.
Stanley, L. (ed.) (1984) *The Diaries of Hannah Cullwick, Victorian Maidservant*, ed. with intro. Liz Stanley, Virago, London.

List B: contemporary diaries

Literary
Bond, M. (ed.) (1948) *The Diaries of Franz Kafka, 1910–1913*, Secker and Warburg, London.
Bond, M. (ed.) (1948) *The Diaries of Franz Kafka, 1914–23*, Secker and Warburg, London.
Olivier Bell, A. (ed.) (1984) *The Diary of Virginia Woolf. Volume 5, 1936–41*, ed. Anne Olivier Bell, Penguin, London.

Social issues
Frank, A. (1997) *The Diary of a Young Girl: the Definitive Edition*, ed. Otto H. Frank and Mirjam Presler, trans. Susan Massotty, Penguin, London.
McCrum, R. (1998) *My Year Off: Rediscovering Life after a Stroke*, Picador, London.

Political
Castle, B. (1980) *The Castle Diaries 1974–76*, Weidenfeld and Nicolson, London.
Crossman, R. (1977) *The Diaries of a Cabinet Minister. Volume Three, Secretary of State for Social Services 1968–70*, Hamilton and Cape, London.

List C: fictional diaries

Defoe

Backsheider, P.R. (ed.) (1992) *Daniel Defoe: a Journal of the Plague Year*, Norton, New York.

Shinagel, M. (ed.) (1994) *Daniel Defoe: Robinson Crusoe*, 2nd edn, Norton, New York.

Gogol

Gogol, N. (1972) *Diary of a Madman and Other Stories*, trans. with intro. R. Wilks, Penguin, London.

Shields

Shields, C. (1994) *The Stone Diaries*, Fourth Estate, London.

Issues which you should consider

1 For each of your three chosen diaries, when and for what purpose was the diary written?
2 Is there any information on how each published version relates to the original text?
3 How is each narrative structured and presented?
4 Can you identify the ways in which authenticity of each is claimed and established?
5 What are the similarities between the three texts you have read?
6 What are the differences between the three texts you have read?

2

Researching Diaries

Diaries tell the truth, the partial truth, and a lot more beside the truth ... In them, you seek – and often find – an atmosphere, a sense of mood of the moment, which could not be acquired in any other way. They should never, ever, be taken as the last word. But as raw material for reconstruction of the past they are as invaluable as they are savagely entertaining. (Pimlott, 2002, p. 2)

Key aims
- To examine the ways in which diaries have been and can be used for social research.

Key objectives
- To consider the different ways in which social research projects can be designed and the implications of different designs for diary research.
- To examine the use of diaries in experimental and social survey research, historical research and naturalistic research.

Research designs and strategies

Each research project has its own unique purpose. Researchers should use methods of data collection and analysis which will enable them to achieve their purpose efficiently, effectively and in a way which is considered acceptable by the users of their research. To avoid reinventing the wheel and to demonstrate the credibility of their research, researchers can make use of established research designs and strategies.

Blaikie (2000, p. 40) in his text on research design asserted that there are well-established social science research designs and identified 12 different designs:

- experiment
- survey
- fieldwork/ethnography
- comparative/historical
- case study
- content analysis
- secondary analysis
- observation
- simulation and gaming
- evaluation research
- social impact research
- action research.

Denzin and Lincoln (2000, p. 20) in the introduction to their *Handbook of Qualitative Research* defined nine 'research strategies':

- study design
- case study
- ethnography, participant observation, performance ethnography
- phenomenology, ethnomethodology
- grounded theory
- life history
- historical method
- action and applied research
- clinical research.

Given the emphasis of their text on qualitative research, experimental and survey research were notable absences from their list.

It is not the purpose of this study to review research designs *per se* but to consider how diary research can be used within different research designs. Therefore in this chapter I will concentrate on four contrasted designs that are important within social research – experimental, social survey, historical, and ethnographic or naturalistic research – and the ways in which diaries can be used within these designs.

Experiments and social surveys are based on primary data, i.e. data collected for the purposes of the research. In both there is an emphasis on the scientific role of the research and a concern to minimise extraneous factors that are not relevant to the research and cause bias. The main emphasis is usually on deduction or testing, which begins with:

> a hypothesis derived from social theory which is then tested against empirical observations and then subsequently used to confirm or refute the original theoretical proposition. (Brewer, 2003d, p. 67)

Experimental and survey researchers can use diaries to overcome one major cause of bias: recall or memory problems. Historical research relies extensively on the use of secondary sources – information which has been recorded in various forms, often for purposes other than research, and is reused by the researcher to provide an understanding of past events, actions, relations and social formations. Historical researchers can use diaries as an additional source of data or as a prime source of evidence when other sources are suppressed or the focus is on a specific individual or group of individuals. Ethnographic or naturalistic research relies on primary data. It exploits the relationship which the researcher establishes with the participants in the research and their willingness to trust and share their lives with the researcher. Ethnographers can use diaries to gain privileged access to the lives of the individuals and communities they are studying and their own journals or fieldnotes can provide important insight into the ways in which their understanding and relationships developed.

Box 2.1 Key issues which researchers need to consider when selecting research designs (developed from Blaikie, 2000, p. 42)

Research design

- *What* will be studied?
- *Why* will it be studied?
- *How* will it be studied?

Selecting research strategy and methods

- *What* research strategy will be used?
- *Where* will the data come from?
- *How* will the data be collected and analysed?

Using diaries

- *How* relevant are diaries for the overall purpose of the research?
- *How* can diaries form part of the research strategies?
- *Can* diaries provide a valuable source of data?
- *What* are the benefits and drawbacks of using diaries compared to other methods of accessing information?

Diaries in experimental and survey research

Experimental and survey designs

In both experimental and survey designs researchers tend to adopt the role of the neutral scientist who is concerned with recording and analysing facts. This approach is more clearly developed in experimental and quasi-experimental research in which the researcher seeks to use facts to test theories and hypotheses:

> *Experimental* designs test casual relations by randomly assigning individuals or entities to experimental and control groups and then applying different procedures or treatments to these groups. *Quasi-experimental* designs also test casual relationships by using some compromise on random assignment to the experimental or control groups. (italics in the original: Blaikie, 2000, p. 41)

In survey research the researcher collects facts to increase understanding and explanation of social phenomena such as voting behaviour or lifestyle choices. Surveys can be used to formulate hypotheses as well as test them (Moser and Kalton, 1971). Wells, in an early poverty survey, defined his social survey as a:

> Fact-finding study dealing chiefly with working-class poverty and the nature of problems of the community. (cited in Moser and Kalton, 1971, p. 1)

Marsh noted that social surveys involve collecting and analysing data in a specific way and she defined a survey as:

> an investigation where:
>
> (a) systematic measurements are made over a series of cases yielding a rectangle of data;
> (b) the variables in the matrix are analysed to see if they show any patterns;
> (c) the subject matter is social. (1982, p. 6)

In both experimental research and social survey there are circumstances in which the use of methods such as observation or interview is restricted and diaries provide an important source of data.

Use of diaries in experiments

In medical research, experimental designs such as randomised controlled trials (RCTs) are designed to measure the impact which specific interventions have on a treatment group and compare this with a matched control group. For many medical researchers the RCT is the gold standard of research (Cochrane, 1972) and the Cochrane database of RCTs records about a third of a million a year (Lilford and Stevens, 2001, p. 8). The emphasis is on identifying observable and measurable differences. Most studies use researchers' objective physiological measures or assessments to assess the impact of treatment on outcomes. For example, RCTs on hypertension used a diastolic blood pressure of 90 mmHg and above as the criterion of entry and then tested the hypothesis that life could be prolonged through the use of hypotensive drugs to reduce blood pressure below that level (Cochrane, 1972, p. 49).

In studies which focus on chronic illnesses such as asthma, not only is it difficult for researchers to observe and record the changing physiological indicators but other outcomes such as the individuals' own feelings of pain or fatigue are important. Furthermore patients' experience of pain and feelings at the time of any investigation or interview may bias their recall (Stone, et al., 2003, p. 182). Diaries can be used to overcome memory or recall problems. As Stone and his colleagues noted:

> By limiting recall and capturing experience close to the time of its occurrence, diaries are thought to produce more accurate and less biased data. Diaries are currently used for the collection of medical symptoms in many therapeutic categories, particularly those where the symptoms are subjective and/or variable. Indeed, it is estimated that diaries are used to collect data in 25% of all phase II–IV pharmaceutical trials. (2003, p. 182)

Parkin and his colleagues (2004) showed that diaries were an effective way of capturing the symptoms associated with multiple sclerosis and could therefore be used to evaluate the impact of beta interferon therapy on individuals who had relapsing-remitting multiple sclerosis. Patients recorded their own assessment of symptoms plus their own measurements of physiological indicators. Hyland and his colleagues (1993) undertook a similar study of asthma patients, inviting them to record physiological data such as peak expiratory flow.

Use of diaries in surveys

Marsh noted many surveys use one-off interviews or questionnaires that include memory questions such as 'Have any of your family had a serious accident in the last year?' (1982, p. 82). She maintained that respondents' ability to recall even quite major events could not be relied on, as telescoping occurs in which individuals allocate to a period an accident which occurred outside the period.

Diaries have been used in surveys of areas such as household expenditure and accidents to overcome memory problems. In the United Kingdom the Expenditure and Food Survey, originally known as the Family Expenditure Survey, has since 1957 been using diaries to monitor the expenditure of households. The Expenditure and Food Survey is based on a voluntary survey of private households which are defined as 'a group of people living at the same address with common housekeeping' (Botting, 2003, p. 162). Expenditure on major items is assessed by a household interview but all other expenditure is assessed using diaries kept by household members:

> Each individual aged 16 or over in the household visited is asked to keep diary records of daily expenditure for two weeks. Information about regular expenditure, such as rent and mortgage payments, is obtained from a household interview along with retrospective information on certain large, infrequent expenditures such as those on vehicles. Since 1998–99 the results have also included information from simplified diaries kept by children aged between 7 and 15. (2003, p. 162)

There are also examples of the use of diaries in *ad hoc* surveys. For example Sissons Joshi and her colleagues (2001) used diaries to examine the risks – accidents and near-misses – which road users experienced in and around the city of Oxford in England. The study recruited through major local employers: 577 employees agreed to keep diaries and 299 returned their diaries. The diaries were a rich source for incidents. Diarists recorded 727 incidents, an average of 2.5 per diarist (2001, pp. 264–5).

Diaries and concealed actions

Experimental and survey research often uses diaries to overcome recall problems. However there are other reasons why conventional data collection techniques may be difficult to use. The behaviour which the researcher wishes to access may be seen as discrediting and therefore individuals may wish to conceal such behaviour. One such area is sexual behaviour. Since the development of the HIV/AIDS epidemic, sexual behaviour, especially risky or 'unsafe' sex, has attracted considerable attention. A major programme of research in this area, Project SIGMA (2003), used sexual diaries to provide insight into and information on gay and bisexual men's sexual activity and the contexts within which it occurred (Coxon, 1996). The project used diaries to overcome the disadvantages of conventional methods such as interviews:

- The diary method was more 'natural', as 'it exists in common social practice' and is 'written in natural language'.
- The data were more accurate, as the diary 'is designed to minimize recall and memory errors and cognitive strain'.
- The information was more detailed and precise in terms of both context, such as the sort of partners or setting, and actual activities (1996, p. 21).

The project built up a dataset of diaries kept by men who have sex with men and used this dataset to explore patterns of behaviour. Coxon and his colleagues used data from 1035 diarists covering 2182 individual diary months, and from a subset of 628 diary months which included one or more acts of anal intercourse, to explore the amount of risk activity, the number of men engaging in a given risk activity and the riskiness of sexual sessions (Coxon and McManus, 2000, p. 2). From their diary data they concluded that a small group of active men accounted for a large percentage of the recorded anal intercourse. However these 'active' men tended to be prepared and use protection. A high proportion of the 'risky' sex involved individuals who had anal intercourse infrequently as they tended not to be prepared (2000, p. 5).

Comment

While diaries can be used in experimental or survey research, they tend not to be the dominant or main source of data. Experimental research relies heavily on observational techniques while surveys tend to use interviews or questionnaires to access data. Generally diaries are used to supplement and overcome the limitations of these methods, especially recall or memory problems, and when such methods are unlikely to access the desired data. When diaries are used in experimental or survey research, the diarist acts as an agent making observations and recording data on behalf of the researcher.

Box 2.2 Key issues which researchers should explore when considering the use of diaries in experimental and social survey research

- What are the main aims and characteristics of experimental and social survey research?
- What are the disadvantages of using diaries in experimental and social survey research designs?
- What are the advantages of using diaries in experimental and social survey research designs?
- In what circumstances do diaries provide access to data that other methods cannot?
- What are the limitations of using diaries and how can they be overcome?

Historical methods and diaries

History can be defined as a study of the past (Jordanova, 2000, p. 1) and is based on the interpretation of sources especially records – mainly written documents but also audio or video recordings, objects and images of the past, which may be collected and stored in and accessed from archives (2000, pp. 28–33). As Jones noted:

> Documentary evidence is the raw material of the historian, whose interpretation of the past is constructed through a careful sifting of many documents of varying kinds: official government records, parliamentary debates, political speeches and election manifestos, mass opinion or surveys, diaries and memoirs, private correspondence, oral testimony, and statistical data. Increasingly, historians have to come to terms with visual evidence as well: propaganda, cartoons, photographs, and advertisements. (1994, p. 5)

Thus diaries form one source of evidence among many. For many researchers, the personal nature of diaries makes them an unreliable and biased source. Seldon notes:

> Diaries, it should be remembered, are just one person's record, often jotted down in haste, of feelings at a particular point in time. At worst, they are dull, plodding and misleading; at best, as with Adrian Mole's, witty, colourful and full of insight. (1994, p. 29)

Traditionally historical research has been concerned with identifying objective facts about historical events and people, especially political events and political elites (Postan, 1971, p. 50). The focus of historical research has expanded with the recognition that historical research not only uses but also creates narratives, i.e. specific situated interpretations of the past (Jordanova, 2000, p. 156). The scope of historical research has also broadened to encompass groups, activities and events outside political elites. Within this broader approach, diaries provide an important source of information. As Jordanova indicated, there is actually a strong fit between historical research and diaries, for both use and to ascribe meaning to time:

> The basic measures of time – hours, days, weeks, months and years – were not invented by historians. But they use them as fundamental, taken-for-granted tools, and give them meaning by assigning additional tags to them, as Daniel Defoe did when he wrote *Journal of the Plague Year*, an account of the Great Plague of 1665 by an invented eyewitness. (2000, p. 114)

Thus it is possible to identify the use of diaries within a variety of aspects of historical research, including relatively traditional research on political events, as well as research on groups traditionally neglected in such research and even ethnographic research on culture contact.

Political research

Diaries can form a valuable source of information when other sources have been restricted by, for example, state censorship. During the second half of the seventeenth century in England, the restored monarchy exerted strong control over the media and therefore diaries such as Pepys's and Evelyn's form a valuable source on both political events and social changes. In the twentieth century diaries have also provided a valuable source of information. Paradoxically the increase in public access to information has made politicians more self-conscious and resulted in considerable self-censorship. Tosh noted the value of diaries in this context:

> In the 1920s ... the select publications of official records grew out of all proportion, as governments strove to excuse themselves, and blame others, for responsibility for the First World War ... Ministers and civil servants, especially those concerned with foreign policy, became more inhibited in their official correspondence; what they wrote to each other privately, or recorded in their diaries, therefore gains in interest ... the vast majority of the diaries and letters available to the historian were written without thought of a wider readership. Of all sources they are the most spontaneous and unvarnished, revealing both the calculated stratagems and unconscious assumptions of public figures. (1984, p. 40)

Diaries and other personal documents form an important source for case studies which focus on specific decisions or events. For example Bale (1999) used a variety of sources including published diaries and memoirs to explore economic decision-making in the Labour government in the mid 1960s. Using these sources he was able to show how in 1964 ministers' personal convictions, plus their perceptions of the electoral unpopularity of devaluation, meant that they resisted strong economic pressure to devalue. In contrast, the changed political circumstances after the government's victory in 1966, plus changed personal perceptions, created the context for devaluation in 1967.

Diaries are an important source for political biographies, which can be seen as historical case studies. Gladstone, a major nineteenth century politician, kept a diary for over 71 years, making an entry for nearly every day between July 1825 and December 1896 (Beales, 1982). Morley (1903), who published a major three-volume biography, had access to and published extracts from the diary. However other scholars were denied access because of the diary's 'introspections, its spiritual misgivings and self accusations and … the fact that the confessions of human weakness are definitely connected with the other sex' (Herbert to Henry Gladstone, cited in Beales, 1982, p. 463). In particular the diary revealed 'not only the extent and some of the ramifications of Gladstone's work to reclaim prostitutes, but also his practice of self-flagellation' (1982, p. 463).

Gladstone's diaries are a rich source of evidence for his attitude to and influence on specific political developments. Beales himself noted some of these areas, for example the development of Anglo-Irish relations and especially Gladstone's changing view on the role of the established Anglican Church in Ireland. Gladstone wrote on 19 June 1845 which he marked secret:

> Keep religion entire, and you secure at least to the individual man his refuge. Ask therefore on every occasion not what best maintains the religious repute of the State but what is least menacing to the integrity of Catholic belief & the Catholic Church. (1982, p. 466)

Social and anthropological research

Political history tends to be top-down history which focuses on the role and development of political elites. The specific impact of 'great men' such as Gladstone, and the privileged access which personal documents such as diaries give to personal developments, perceptions and motives, are important for understanding political decisions and events. However increasingly historians and social scientists working with historical sources have focused on broader social processes and on groups who are relatively excluded or only exceptionally given voice in the official record.

Social history is concerned with the ways in which social relations and structures are formed within specific societies at specific times. The emphasis tends to be on groups who are excluded from traditional historical narratives. This is reflected in the growth of oral history in which interview techniques are used to access evidence from excluded individuals and communities. For example Redlich (1975) argued that autobiographical sources such as memoirs and diaries were rich sources of data which have been neglected by historians and should be used to develop a fuller understanding of the ways in which small social changes contributed to more fundamental changes. MacFarlane (1970, p. 3) has asserted that materials such as diaries can make a major contribution to understanding the past by overcoming the limitations inherent in other records.

Some well-known diaries have contributed to social history. For example, Pepys's diary provided substantial information about both working conditions in the emerging civil service and domestic relations. Westhauser (1994) has compared Pepys's diary with that kept by Adam Eyre. Westhauser noted that friendship and marriage made competing demands on men in the seventeenth century. High status men who had made good marriages tended to use their own homes as a basis for sociability and hospitality. Lower status men and those with 'bad' marriages tended to use public houses. Both Adam Eyre and Samuel Pepys were men of the 'middling sort' who were rising to prominence at the end of the seventeenth century; social change had implications for their sociability and their relationships with their wives, with a move from meeting in public houses to meeting in their own homes.

One group often excluded from the historical record are women, and there has been substantial use of diaries in both studying the life history of women and exploring their roles and relationships. Botankie (1999) noted that in seventeenth century England the Protestant duty of self-examination stimulated diary writing among women as well as men and this enabled women to pursue a male activity, writing, as well as to expand into other areas of male activity such as providing spiritual guidance. However such activity was restricted to the elite until there was wider access to requisite resources for keeping a diary in nineteenth century industrial societies (see for example Huff's 1985 bibliography of nineteenth century women's manuscript diaries).

Huff (1985) used diaries to explore the ways in which Victorian women constructed childbirth and motherhood. She argued that excessive reliance on fictional sources for personal and emotional responses to childbirth has meant that images of women as devils or angels have persisted. She showed that Victorian women used their diaries to record the details of their pregnancy and childbirth and that such practices helped develop relationships between women sharing the same experiences. These diaries could also be used as sources of information on parturition and disease.

Diaries provide a rich source of data for researchers who wish to explore the development of an individual life, and the activities and relationships of particular groups in society. The utility of diaries may be restricted by their availability but it may be possible to minimise such limitations by seeing an individual diarist or group of diarists as typical or representative of a wider group. Diaries can be used to access information within a specific society or social group and to explore the relationships between groups and even between cultures in historical anthropology.

Historical anthropology can be seen as a form of social history that deals with the development and interactions of cultures. An emphasis on culture involves a particular interest in the development of the collective mental life of groups and the ways in which they perceive and mentally organise the world they live in.

MacFarlane used Ralph Josselin's diary to 'step back 300 years and to look out through the eyes of an Essex vicar of the mid seventeenth century' (1970, p. 11). MacFarlane examined the demographic and social issues, such as Josselin's relationship with his kin, godparents, servants and neighbours. However he was more interested in the cultural dimensions of these relationships and the diarist's life. He noted that:

> The use of a diary as a prime source, rather than the parish registers or probate inventories upon which most social history is at present based, allows us to make a more personal and intimate study. It enables us to probe a long-vanished mental world, as well as to describe the social characteristics of a previous civilization. (1970, p. 3)

MacFarlane developed a picture of Josselin's mental world, especially the importance of religious and magical thinking evident *inter alia* in the millenarian images associated with the Second Coming in his diary:

> This mental world, so full of omens and symbolic nuances, contained few barriers against rumours of witchcraft and the millennium, of monstrous births and meetings with the devil. Analysis of the Josselin family's dreams has already shown that during the 1650s they dreamt fairly frequently of strange fires and figures in the sky, which seemed to fit in with the prophecies in the Book of Revelation concerning the Second Coming. (1970, p. 190)

Sahlins (1995) also used diaries for a historical ethnography seeking to explain how native Hawaiian islanders made sense of an unprecedented event, their first encounter with Europeans. Sahlins used a variety of diaries and other documents kept by Captain Cook and his crew and compared them with oral traditions and histories from the islands. Sahlins argued that the islanders tried to make sense of the situation by using their experience and understanding of the world to interpret the new situation. The best fit between the new situation and previous experience was that Cook was an incarnation of the god Lono and this interpretation played an important role in events, especially Cook's death.

The starting point for Cook's analysis was the accounts of events in the various diaries. Sahlins started with an account published by Heinrich Zimmermann, a German seaman who kept notes in German. He used these notes to publish his own version of the voyage, which appeared in 1781 before the Admiralty's official version in 1784:

> Zimmermann's text indicates he was present – 'We held the five boats at a short distance from the land' – and reports one of the interviews [between the party sent to recover Cook's body and the islanders]. The Hawaiians, he wrote, 'showed us a piece of white cloth as a countersign of peace but mocked at ours and answered as follows: "O-runa no

te tuti Heri te moi a popo Here mai" which means: "The god Cook is dead but sleeps in the woods and will come tomorrow."'... The Hawaiian here is again decipherable, but is more straightforward than Zimmermann's translation: 'Cook is indeed Lono; he is going to sleep; tomorrow he will come' – no death, no woods. The apparently curious statement fits into the range of European accounts of the incident, all of which cite Hawaiians to the effect that Cook would return the next day. (1995, p. 18)

Sahlins supported this analysis with a review of the events of Cook's visit to Hawaii in 1778 and 1779. He noted that there was documentary evidence that Cook was greeted in Hawai'i island as a personification of the New Year god Lono (1995, p. 20). Sahlins argued that events associated with Cook's visit and his death provided insight into the islanders' rationality, the way they thought about the world at the time. This rationality included the possibility that in certain circumstances gods, humans and natural entities such as winds shared characteristics and could have a common identity. Therefore it was not irrational for the islanders to see and treat Cook as a manifestation of one of their gods.

Both MacFarlane and Sahlins show the sophisticated ways in which diaries can be used to explore the culture and mindsets of past social groups. This is particularly challenging in the case of other cultures where some of the evidence is embedded and has to be deciphered from the diary, as in the case of the Cook voyage diaries. However, in such research it is important that the interpretation is supported from other sources such as oral traditions which themselves may be recorded in travellers' or missionaries' journals or anthropologists' fieldnotes.

Comment

Diaries are a valuable and comparatively neglected resource for historical research. They can provide supporting evidence for traditional political histories. In social and anthropological studies that use historical data they are a unique source offering a way of accessing information that could not be accessed in any other way.

Box 2.3 Key issues which researchers should explore when considering the use of diaries in historical research

- What are the main aims and characteristics of historical research?
- What are the disadvantages of using diaries in historical research designs?
- What are the advantages of using diaries in historical research designs?
- In what circumstances do diaries provide access to data that other methods cannot?

Using diaries for naturalistic research

While research designs such as social surveys provide cost-effective ways of collecting large bodies of data, the explanatory value of these data is often limited. While survey research is good at describing what people do, it is rather less effective at explaining or understanding why they do it. Accessing individuals' interpretations of their world is the only way to do this. As Porter has noted in a review of qualitative analysis in nursing research, the premise of naturalistic research is that:

> the social world we live in can only be understood through an understanding of the meanings and motives that guide social actions and interactions of individuals ... Qualitative analysis is concerned with describing the actions and interactions of research subjects in a certain context, and with interpreting the motivations and understandings that lie behind those actions. (2000, p. 399)

Researchers can access these types of data by becoming part of the 'natural setting' (Fielding, 1993) and participating in the social life of the people who are being researched. The aim of naturalistic research is to study the world as far as possible in a state that is not contaminated by the research process, so that '"natural" not "artificial" settings, like experiments or formal interviews, should be the primary source of data' (Hammersley and Atkinson, 1995, p. 6). Naturalistic researchers are committed to seeing the world from the social actors' point of view, and to do this they seek to participate in the everyday life of a community so that they can see the world from the point of view of a member of the community. Blaikie described the chief characteristic of this approach in the following way:

> [It] is a commitment to viewing the social world – social actions and events – from the viewpoints(s) of the people being studied. This commitment involves discovering *their* socially constructed reality and penetrating the frames of meaning within which they conduct their activities. (italics in the original: 2000, p. 251)

Diaries provide an important and often neglected source of data for naturalistic researchers, as they can be seen as documents of life which 'give "voice" to other people' (Plummer, 1983, p. 1). While there is a variety of such documents, Plummer noted that:

> The diary is the document of life *par excellence,* chronicling as it does the immediately contemporaneous flow of public and private events that are significant to the diarist. The word 'contemporary' is very crucial here, for each diary entry – unlike life histories – is sedimented into a particular moment in time. (italics in the original: 2001, p. 48)

Diaries are particularly suited to a naturalistic approach as they facilitate 'the examination of reported events and experiences in their natural, spontaneous context' (Bolger et al., 2003, p. 580).

Diaries providing insight into taken-for-granted activities

Diaries can be used to access those facets of social life which members of social groups take for granted and are therefore not easily articulated or accessed through research methods such as interviews. Interactions within social groups imply common and shared characteristics, for example members of the groups can competently speak the same language and have sufficient agreement about the nature of the world to facilitate meaningful communication and interaction. The shared agreements or tacit knowledge about the world which Schutz (1971) called 'common sense' tend to be internalised through the processes of socialisation.

Diaries can be used to access such tacit knowledge. For example Robinson (1971) generated insight into the ways in which people decided they or significant others were ill. While he identified some elements of formal explicit decision-making, much assessment was grounded in tacit knowledge. Robinson noted that for the most part actors did not consider more than one course of action and responded with 'no thinking out and weighing up of alternative strategies' (1971, p. 36). So when faced with familiar situations people used their common sense; they 'knew what to do and did it' (1971, p. 36). In addition to household interviews, the wife or mother in each household was invited to complete a diary for a four-week period and 20 did so. Robinson used these diaries to identify patterns which indicated how individuals made sense of their situation and did or did not invoke the concept of 'illness' in this process. In particular he identified an 'incubation' stage during which the diarist recorded concerns about his or her health or those of a household member. These concerns then led into a decision to seek help which either resolved the matter or led to further action. For example he noted how Mrs S. who was a pregnant woman with a two-year-old child, used her diary to document a series of concerns about her health and to record how these concerns were resolved by a visit to an antenatal clinic (see Figure 2.1).

Diaries as a means of providing insight into the ways in which individuals perceive and interpret situations

Diaries can be used not only to identify patterns of behaviour but also to provide greater insight into how individuals interpret situations and ascribe meanings to actions and events and therefore how actions that may appear irrational to outsiders are rational to the diarist.

Merton and his colleagues (1957) used diaries in their classic study of the education and socialisation of medical students. They examined the ways in which the students perceived and evaluated their situation and how the formal and explicit parts of their learning interacted with informal learning and the overall shaping of their attitudes to medicine and patients. Initially four and

Day	Symptom	Action taken	Comment
1	My nails are splitting badly		
2	Nothing		
3	My legs are swelling badly		Wish I had time to rest my legs more
4	My legs still swelling and nails splitting. I have had a lot of constipation lately	Taken laxative for constipation	
5	I still have Wednesday's symptoms		
6	I still have the same symptoms		
7	My body is feeling very weak and my nerves are still bad		
8	Just the same as Sat.		
9	I have constipation	Taken laxatives	
10	I had very bad back and stomach pains before the laxatives work		
11	I had very bad wind in my back, eating far too much last week or so. But just can't stop myself	Had J. [husband] to rub my back until wind came up	
12	Now I have haemorrhoids	I went to antenatal clinic. Told doctor my symptoms	Doctor told me I am overweight and must stop eating too much
13	Nothing		
14	Nothing		
15	Nothing		
16	Nothing		
17	Nothing		
18	Nothing		
19	Nothing		

Figure 2.1   *Extract from a family health diary (Robinson, 1971, p. 31)*

subsequently two students in each of the four years of the training course kept a 'detailed journal'. One of the research team read each weekly instalment of each diary to identify:

> tentative hypotheses about the distinctive aspects of the social environment and their significance for processes of attitudinal and cognitive learning. (Merton, 1957, p. 46)

Since these hypotheses were explored through 'intensive interviews' with the student diarists, little of the original diary material made it through to the final analysis. For example, Fox's (1957) analysis of the ways in which student physicians learnt to deal with the uncertainties inherent in medical practice relied heavily on data from the 'intensive interviews'. The only acknowledged direct quotations from the diaries come in the methodology section where Merton provided two extracts from diaries to illustrate how two students presented the same event, a below average mark in a chemistry examination, in different ways:

> *Student A*: Monday, we got back our chem. Exams. As I supposed, I did flunk it. The marks in general were good; most folks about me got high 80's and 90's. *I guess some of us are just naturally born stupid and careless.*
>
> *Student B*: Well, we got our chemistry tests today. I didn't do as well as I should have, but I passed with a very high C ... I really knew about a B's worth of material ... I seemed to see a lot of 100's and 90's floating around the lab, but what can you do about that? *So many of the fellows were chemistry majors and/or took elementary biochemistry in undergraduate school.* (italics in the original: 1957, p. 45)

Diaries and ethnography

Naturalistic research underpins ethnographic designs that were initially developed for the anthropological study of other cultures. Since Malinowski pioneered intensive fieldwork techniques by leaving the safety of the colonial enclave and living with and sharing the lives of Trobriand islanders in the 1910s, anthropologists have been committed to naturalistic research. Fieldnotes form a central component of fieldwork and these take the form of the researcher's contemporaneous record of observations and reflections, in other words a journal or diary:

> Field notes are the bricks and mortar of an ethnographic edifice. These notes consist primarily of data from interviews and daily observations ... Fieldwork inundates the ethnographer with information, ideas, and events. Ethnographic work is exhausting, and the fieldworker will be tempted to stop taking notes or to postpone typing the day's hieroglyphics each night. Memory fades quickly, however, and unrecorded information will soon be overshadowed by subsequent events. Too long a delay sacrifices the rich immediacy of concurrent notes. (Fetterman, 1998, p. 114)

Similarly Emerson and his colleagues note that 'the ethnographer writes down in regular, systematic ways what she observes and learns while participating in the daily rounds of life of others' (1995, p. 1).

In de Munck's (1998) account of the life of a Sri Lankan village, he described how he observed and interpreted the conflicts between members of the village. The raw data for his analysis were two notebooks, which he used to maintain a daily record. One of these notebooks he classified as official as it included his formal records, his 'field jottings, maps, diagrams, interviews and observations' whereas the other was an 'unofficial' notebook that contained his personal reflections, 'mullings, questions, comments, quirky notes, and diary type entries' (1998, p. 45).

Anthropologists use fieldnote journals as the material for their accounts of the people they study. It is possible to use both the journals and published ethnographies to gain insight into the process. Malinowski's accounts have been subjected to particular scrutiny. He was a pioneer of fieldwork and his books were designed to give readers the feeling that they were participating in the lives of the people he studied. In the preface to *Coral Gardens and Their Magic* he states that:

> In this book we are going to meet the essential Trobriander. Whatever he might appear to others, to himself he is first and foremost a gardener. His passion for the soil is that of a real peasant. He experiences a mysterious joy in delving into the earth, in turning it up, planting the seed, watching the plant grow, mature, and yield the desired harvest. If you want to know him, you must meet him in his yam garden, among his palm groves or on his taro fields. (Malinowski, 1966, p. xix)

Surprisingly there is little evidence that Malinowski's fieldnotes have been re-examined. Uberoi (1971) reworked Malinowski's analysis of the Kula ring, stressing its political role in a competitive environment that lacked the moderating influence of centralised political authority, but he used published ethnographic accounts not original fieldnotes. However the diaries which Malinowski kept while he was doing his fieldwork (Firth, 1989, p. xi) have been published and subjected to analysis, especially by Geertz (1988). Malinowski's *Diary* (1989) provided a rather different account of the development and practice of fieldwork to the conventional version. As Geertz notes, Malinowski's *Diary* showed that he 'did not, in fact, always maintain an understanding and benevolent attitude towards his informants, his state of mind in the field was anything but coolly objective' (1988, p. 112). Malinowski's comments on both islanders and Europeans were often highly judgemental, as can be seen in the following extract:

> Thursday 21 [1918]. Slept a long time – 'catching up on my sleep' – I feel I need it. I feel a little knocked out; but not unwell ... Wrote diary, neglected since departure from

Sanaroa. I must draw up a system of investigation on the Amphletts. In the morning I wrote a long time, started ethnogr. fairly late. Worked first with Anaibutuna and Tovasana [Tovasana was the main headman in the Amphletts; Malinowski was staying in his village, Nu'agasi on Gumasila, and used him as an informant (see *Argonauts of the Western Pacific*, particularly Chapter XI) (editor's notes)] who are not bad, *but not first-class informants*. After lunch Kipela and an old man; I got annoyed with the latter and chased him away. For a moment I was afraid that this would spoil my business, then Kipela successfully resolved the difficulties. (emphases in the original: 1989, pp. 228–9).

Geertz (1988) has analysed Malinowski's *Diary* and his other published work as texts. He has identified an oscillation in Malinowski's texts between two images, that of a scientific observer, 'a figure … rigorously objective, dispassionate, thorough, exact, and disciplined … and dedicated to wintery truth', and that of a compassionate and skilled fellow human being who has 'enlarged capacities for adaptability and fellow feeling, for insinuating himself into practically any situation, as to be able to see as savages see, think as savages think, and on occasion even feel as they feel and believe as they believe' (1988, p. 79). He argued that Malinowski constructed his text in this way so that he could overcome the fundamental problem of ethnography, creating an intelligible and persuasive account of another culture:

> The problem … is to represent the research process in the research product; to write ethnography in such a way as to bring one's interpretations of some society, culture, way of life, or whatever and one's encounters with some of its members, carriers, representatives, or whomever into an intelligible relationship. Or … it is to get an I-witnessing author into a they-picturing story. To commit oneself to an essentially biographical conception of Being There, rather than a reflective, an adventural, or an observational one, is to commit oneself to text-building. (1988, p. 84)

Geertz identified this diary approach to ethnography in other texts including Read's (1965) account of life in Highland New Guinea. He noted that while Read presented himself in a very different way, he shared with Malinowski the same confessional approach to creating ethnographic texts:

> Instead of the Dostoevskian darkness and Conradian blur [of Malinowski's text], the Readian 'I' is filled with confidence, rectitude, tolerance, patience, good nature, energy, enthusiasm, optimism – with an almost palpable determination to do what is right and think what is proper. If the *Diary* presents the image of the womanizing café intellectual cast among savages, *The High Valley* presents one of an indefinite country vicar. (1988, p. 85)

Geertz's textual approach to ethnographic narrative provides one way of exploring how such narratives are constructed and used and has stimulated an interesting interaction between textual analysis and social sciences. Diaries form an important source of data for such analyses and such analyses can contribute to our understanding of the ways in which diaries work as texts. I will therefore return to these issues when I consider the analysis of diary evidence in Chapter 5.

Comment

Given the stated aim of researchers using a naturalistic approach is to study individuals and communities in their natural setting and to minimise intrusion, diaries offer an attractive source of information. Since diarists control the recording of information, diaries appear to offer privileged access to the diarist's perceptions and world. This characteristic has made them attractive as a way of exploring tacit knowledge that is difficult to articulate in, for example, interviews because such knowledge is grounded in taken-for-granted assumptions about the nature of the world. While diaries may be seen as a means to an end, they can also be seen as texts in their own right used by the diarist to construct his or her own identity to support an account of social reality. The nature and structure of such accounts can be explored using techniques developed in literary or textual analysis.

Box 2.4 Key issues which researchers should explore when considering the use of diaries in naturalistic research

- What are the main aims and characteristics of naturalistic research?
- What sources and texts are available and how would diaries add to these sources?
- What are the advantages of using diaries in naturalistic designs?
- In what circumstances do diaries provide access to data that other methods cannot?

Summary and comment

Diaries can be used in a wide variety of research designs. In experimental and survey research, they can be used either to overcome the recall problems present in synchronic techniques of collecting data, such as the one-off interview, or to explore areas of human life concealed from investigation such as sexual relations between men. In historical research, diaries provide a valuable source of information, which can both supplement other sources and for some purposes and in some circumstances form a key source. Diaries form an important source for the development of life histories and biographies that are used in traditional political history as well as in social history. Diaries can also play a part in developing anthropological histories and providing insight into other cultures, whether these are in seventeenth century rural England or eighteenth century Hawaii. For research using a naturalistic approach, diaries provide an important resource. While it is clear that diaries in the form of field-notes have formed a key part of ethnographic fieldwork since Malinowski's pioneering work in the 1910s, it is not clear that the full potential of diaries is recognised in this area.

KEY POINTS

Overall

- Diaries can be used in a range of research designs.
- Diaries can be used on their own or in combination with other methods.
- Diaries provide a means of accessing hard-to-reach groups or activities.

Experimental/survey

- Diaries can be used where there are practical problems in making suitable observations, because the relevant events or activities are rare or difficult to observe.
- Diarists can act as a surrogate for the researcher in recording data.

Unsolicited/historical

- Unsolicited diaries provide a major source of data, especially when other sources have been censored or are absent.
- Historical research using diaries is restricted to those periods when diary keeping was established and for those groups among whom diary keeping was a regular habit.

Naturalistic/ethnographic

- Diaries provide a way of accessing data in a relatively natural form and can therefore be used to explore the taken-for-granted aspects of social interaction.

EXERCISE

Diaries have been used in a variety of different research projects with different research designs. To familiarise yourself with diary research and to gain insight into the challenges and opportunities offered by using diaries, you should look at one or more example from each of the types of research identified in lists A, B and C. You should then consider the issues which I have outlined.

Diaries which can be used in the exercise

The diaries are grouped into three categories: experimental/survey, historical/unsolicited, naturalistic/ethnographic.

List A: experimental/survey

Coxon, A.P.M. (1996) *Between the Sheets: Sexual Diaries and Gay Men's Sex in the Era of AIDS*, Cassell, London.
Parkin, D., Rice, N., Jacoby, A. and Doughty, J. (2004) Use of a visual analogue scale in a daily patient diary: modelling cross-sectional time-series data on health-related quality of life, *Social Science and Medicine*, 59, pp. 351–60.

List B: historical/unsolicited

MacFarlane, A. (1970) *The Family Life of Ralph Josselin: a Seventeenth-Century Clergyman. An Essay in Historical Anthropology*, Cambridge University Press, Cambridge.
Pollock, L.A. (1983) *Forgotten Children: Parent–Child Relations from 1500 to 1900*, Cambridge University Press, Cambridge.
Sahlins, M. (1995) *How 'Natives' Think: about Captain Cook, for Example*, University of Chicago Press, Chicago.

List C: naturalistic/ethnographic

Crossley, M.L. (2003) 'Let me explain': narrative emplotment and one patient's experience of oral cancer, *Social Science and Medicine*, 56, pp. 439–48.
Jones, R.H. and Candlin, C.N. (2003) Constructing risk across timescales and trajectories: gay men's stories of sexual encounters, *Health, Risk and Society*, 5, pp. 199–213.

(Continued)

Issues which you should consider

1 Identify the key aims and objectives of each research study.
2 Examine how and in what ways diaries were used to contribute to the achievement of these aims and objectives.
3 Were diaries the sole source of data?
4 If not, consider their relationship with other forms of data collection and their distinctive role.
5 How were the data from the diaries collected and analysed?
6 What contribution did the diaries make to the findings and conclusions of the study?
7 What status was given to the diary data?

3

Getting Started: Finding Diarists and Diaries

Who from the teeming millions of world population is to be selected for such intensive study and social science immortality? (Plummer, 2001, p. 133)

Key aims
- To outline the ways in which the researcher can identify diaries and diarists for their research.

Key objectives
- To examine the issues involved in recruiting for experimental and survey diary research.
- To consider ways in which unsolicited diaries can be located and accessed.
- To examine the issues of engaging participants in naturalistic or ethnographic diary research.

Approaches to selection and recruitment

The ways in which diarists are recruited will depend on the purpose of the research, especially the design which the researcher is using, and the nature of the data which he or she is seeking to access. The selection of cases for inclusion in the research is guided by the specific nature of the design. In this section I will first consider some of these concerns and principles before moving on to consider and give examples of how these choices can and should be made.

Experimental and survey research

In experimental and survey research the researcher is usually seeking to make generalisations about a large population of cases, often in the form of testing a hypothesis about the relationship between specific characteristics or variables of cases (Marsh, 1982, p. 7). In both experimental and survey research, the selection processes need to be carefully managed to ensure the findings can be generalised to the whole population. In both types of research this tends to be done through a random component in the sampling process.

In experimental studies the researcher aims to observe the effects of specific interventions. In studies using human subjects, the experiment usually involves observing the results of an intervention with one group of subjects and then comparing this with the experiences of a control group who have not experienced the intervention. It is important that the two groups are the 'same' and this sameness is usually achieved by randomly allocating potential participants to the experimental and control groups. (1982, p. 7). Lilford and Stevens stressed the importance of such selection processes in medical research in the following way:

> Randomisation provides protection against selection bias – inaccuracy that occurs if patients in treatment and control groups have different capacities to benefit. Randomisation, provided that the allocation is fully concealed, ensures that confounding variables are distributed by chance alone. Blinding prevents the possibility of performance bias ... and outcome bias. (2001, p. 7)

In social surveys researchers have less control in terms of isolating and focusing on key variables or characteristics. Therefore it is intrinsically more difficult to control for confounding factors (Marsh, 1982, p. 7). The starting point for a social survey is the population – all the units or cases which share the characteristics of interest to the researcher (Bryman, 2001, p. 85). Where resources are unlimited or the population is small then the survey may take the form of a census or a 'complete enumeration' of the whole population (Moser and Kalton, 1971, p. 54): for example, in the regular decennial census which has been conducted since 1801 the whole population of the United Kingdom is included (Raftery et al., 2001, p. 139). However in most cases resources are limited and the most effective use of resources is to select and study a smaller group or sample and then to use the data from this group to generalise about the larger population. As in experimental research, a random or chance element can be used in the sampling or selection process to reduce the likelihood of bias undermining the generalisability of the findings. In random sampling 'the inclusion of a unit of the population occurs entirely by chance' (Bryman, 2001, p. 506). Randomness facilitates the use of statistical techniques to provide information about the level of confidence of the findings, i.e. the likelihood that generalisations and relationships really exist and are not the product of chance (Marsh, 1982, pp. 69–97).

In some circumstances, it may not be possible to use straightforward sampling techniques either because it is difficult to precisely define the population or because it is difficult to access a hard-to-reach population. It may be necessary to use other approaches to sampling. For example, snowball sampling can be used to access hard-to-reach populations such as drug misusers (Bryman, 2001, p. 99). The researcher establishes contact with 'a small group of people who are relevant to the research topic and then uses these to establish contacts with others' (2001, p. 98). When using such sampling methods, researchers need to examine how their findings can be generalised.

Naturalistic research

For researchers using naturalistic research, sampling or selection does not have the same importance as in experimental or survey research. Researchers using naturalistic techniques often do not start with a hypothesis to test; instead they begin with something they do not understand, a puzzle about certain patterns of behaviour such as taking harmful drugs or believing in witchcraft. Generalisation does not take the form of making statistical inferences about the characteristics of a population from a representative sample, but rather consists of gaining insight into social processes and the rationality which underpins observed actions and events. In such circumstances it may not be meaningful to talk of sampling; for example Denzin and Lincoln's (2000) text on qualitative research does not have a chapter on sampling. In naturalistic research the concern is to select cases or settings which will provide an opportunity to gain the desired insight. Plummer (2001, p. 133) noted how many life histories resulted from chance encounters. Hammersley and Atkinson (1995, p. 37) also argued that in naturalistic research there is often an element of chance in the initial selection of the research setting. The initial research setting is often just a starting point, and as the research progresses and the researcher identifies key issues through analysis of information, such analysis can be used to select new settings. This approach has been formalised within research designs such as grounded theory, which involves a phased selection of settings with each round of data collection and analysis generating fresh insights that lead to the selection of new settings in which to test out the insights and to fill gaps in the data and theories through 'theoretical sampling' (Charmaz, 2000, p. 519).

Historical research

In historical research researchers access and use documents and records which are relevant to the purposes of their research. As in experimental and survey research, chance plays an important role in the research process. However while experimental and survey researchers deliberately use chance to minimise selection biases, those using historical documents have to acknowledge and manage the random or chance elements built into survival of records. Jordanova observed that:

> Many sources have survived accidentally. They are always vulnerable to mishaps such as fire and flood, they have often been destroyed wilfully, and simple neglect accounts for a great deal of loss. Furthermore many sources have been created with no particular view of their permanence in mind. Although most institutions have deliberately sought, with an eye on the future, to generate accounts of their activities, many other areas of human life are less self-conscious. Even where there have been attempts to leave records for posterity, they remain vulnerable. (2000, pp. 28–9)

Researchers using diaries for historical research cannot control either the scope of diary keeping or the survival of diaries. Essentially they are opportunistic, they have to make do with what is available. The crucial questions relate to what has survived, where it is stored, how easy it is to access and how relevant the diaries are for the purposes of the research. If the focus is on a specific historical case study or on the nature of narratives in specific diaries then the issue of representativeness may not be important. However if the researcher is seeking to generalise from a specific diary or group of diaries to the experiences of a wider group then the researcher needs to explore the typicality or representativeness of the diarist(s). Interpretation is not static but may change as new and additional sources are identified. For example, Jordanova (2000, p. 30) noted the *Diary of Anne Frank* was initially seen as unique and its accidental survival, publication and promotion gave it iconic status (see for example the personal responses of Primo Levi, Nelson Mandela and Eleanor Roosevelt cited in Anne Frank House, n.d.). However recently historians have identified 'other first-hand sources, providing a whole new context' in which to interpret it (Jordanova, 2000, p. 30).

Comment

Getting started in empirical research requires deciding who to involve in the research and why. The choices and decisions have to be made in the context of the purposes and design of the research. In experimental and survey research the importance of generalising from specific cases in the research to the wider population means that researchers use systematic selection procedures that reduce the possibility of bias and therefore unrepresentativeness. Researchers using naturalistic techniques are less concerned with numbers and the technology of selection and more interested in the opportunities to engage individuals and groups who can provide understanding and insight. Researchers using unsolicited diaries need to identify where such diaries are held, whether privately or in archives. Researchers dealing with the recent past may need to engage in search strategies to identify who can provide access to suitable diaries. Researchers dealing with the more distant past have to identify and access archives.

Selecting and recruiting diarists for experimental or survey research

In both experimental and survey research the selection of research subjects is a crucial and vital part of the research process as the research subjects have to meet specified criteria. In experimental contexts these are defined by the nature of the experiment, while in the survey these are defined by the need to generalise from the selected sample to a wider population.

Recruiting subjects for experiments

In experimental research, the main characteristics of the individuals to be included are defined by the nature of the experiment. When using diaries, researchers also have to identify the additional characteristics which will ensure that the diarists maintain an accurate record. Generally diaries are used when the researcher cannot undertake the observations and the diarist acts as the researcher's agent in observing and recording relevant data. For example when monitoring the impact of different treatment regimes on chronic illnesses such as diabetes or multiple sclerosis, the researcher may need the research subject to record not only compliance with the prescribed treatment regime but also relevant clinical data such as blood sugar levels. In this context, the researcher has to recruit subjects who can be trusted to follow the instructions provided by the researcher and keep honest and accurate records.

It is possible to address this issue through three processes:

- through the initial recruitment process
- through training of and support for diarists
- by checking the reliability of entries and where appropriate providing feedback.

In fact these processes are linked: for example if individuals are recruited who do not fully meet the requirements of the study it may be possible through training and support to develop their competence as a diarist. I will consider the recruitment issues in this chapter and the other issues in Chapter 4.

When recruiting diarists, the experimental researcher needs to ensure that the person recruited has the competence to maintain the diary, an understanding of the purposes of maintaining the diary or record and the motivation to keep an accurate record.

COMPETENCE   Traditional diary keeping requires basic competence in record keeping such as literacy (Corti, 2003, p. 72), though the development of recording technology means it is possible to use audio and video equipment for diary keeping. Diary keeping in experiments may require additional skills to those involved in keeping a regular record. For example in maintaining a diary which monitors the ways in which a specific form of treatment influences diabetes, the diarist may need to measure and record blood sugar levels, accurately report symptoms and ensure all recordings are made at the specified time. In effect the diarist needs to acquire the skills which a competent health professional uses to monitor diabetes. The precise skills required will depend on the specific nature of the experiment and the type of information which needs to be recorded.

UNDERSTANDING   Experiments are often set within a positivistic paradigm that involves the 'application of natural science methods and practice to the social sciences' and aspires to use methods that result in certainty, precision and objectivity (Brewer, 2003a, pp. 235–6). It is therefore important to ensure that recording is accurate, precise and regular. If the diarist does not understand the importance of such concepts then it is likely that the experiment will be compromised.

MOTIVATION   Since diary maintenance can be seen as a potentially time consuming or disruptive activity, diarists need to be motivated to ensure that they maintain their diaries in the prescribed way. While competence is likely to develop as the diarist participates in the research, motivation is likely to decline. Motivation may be particularly problematic when the experiment involves compliance with an intervention which the diarist finds intrusive or inconvenient. For example if the intervention in a diabetes study involves a dietary change that the diarists finds difficult to sustain, then the motivation to keep accurate records is likely to be considerably reduced.

Incentives or payments can be used as a way of increasing motivation. Commercial research such as market research or drug trials often involves payments to participants but such payments are less common, even controversial, in non-commercial research. For example in our diary study of stroke survivors we wished to make payments to participants as recognition of the time and effort they had devoted to the project, but the funders felt that such payments were inappropriate (Alaszewski and Alaszewski, 2005). Other researchers using diaries have offered payments: for example in 1992–3 Project SIGMA offered to make a donation of £2 to the Terrence Higgins Trust when they received a successfully completed diary (Coxon, 1999, p. 224), and Jones and his colleagues offered participants in their study 'a stipend of HK$1000 for their ten-week participation' (2000, p. 8). The topic of payments is relatively neglected within the social science literature but has been addressed in the medical research literature (see for example Johns Hopkins Medicine, 2004; Grady, 2001). Payment is ethically acceptable if it does not constitute an undue inducement to participate and

> if it constitutes reasonable reimbursement for time and expenses … [enabling] people to participate in research without excessive cost to themselves, either in expenses, lost wages, or both. (Grady, n.d., p. 1)

Parkin and his colleagues' (2000; 2004) diary study of the effects of beta interferon therapy for people with relapsing-remitting multiple sclerosis provides an example of the ways in which diarists can be recruited for experimental studies. This trial did not include a control, so recruitment was only to the main study group of 62 participants. The team dealt with the motivation issues by approaching a larger group of potential participants so that individuals who were not motivated to participate could refuse. They dealt with the competence and understanding issues by providing training, hand-delivering the initial diary and taking the participant through a model diary entry. The team used the health services in one locality to identify potential participants and used inclusion criteria to define potential recruits:

> [the potential participants] lived within the catchment area of the Neurology Service at Newcastle upon Tyne, United Kingdom. Inclusion criteria were that they were identified by their consultant as appropriate for beta interferon therapy and had not had a relapse, defined as 'appearance of a new symptom or worsening of an existing one sufficient to require management in hospital, either as an inpatient or day case'... The project had a short time scale and we could not collect a truly random sample; those eligible were chosen as they were identified by a research nurse. (2004, pp. 351–2)

Box 3.1 General issues the researcher should consider in recruiting diarists for experimental research

Competence

- What sort of skills will the diarist need?
- How can these skills be assessed?
- How can skills be developed?

Understanding

- What does the diarist need to understand about the study?
- How can understanding be assessed?
- How can understanding be enhanced?

Motivation

- What sort of motivation will the diarist need?
- In what way can it be assessed?
- How can motivation be maintained and enhanced?

Incentives

- Would it be appropriate to provide reasonable reimbursement for time and expenses?
- What sort of reimbursement should be provided?
- What level of reimbursement is appropriate?

The research team explored the potential bias involved in this recruitment process, comparing the characteristics of the 62 participants with those of the national population and arguing that they were consistent and so there was no obvious bias. They argue that 'overall performance of the diaries was very good, including high completion rates and good quality' (2004, pp. 351–2); 39 respondents (63%) recorded complete information, which meant every entry every day.

Recruiting participants for surveys

Issues of competence, understanding and motivation are also relevant when recruiting diarists for social surveys. However diarists' engagement with surveys is likely to be more limited and less demanding as surveys are not designed to impact on the diarist in the same way as experiments. The way in which participants are selected is crucially important in a survey. In experiments such as clinical trials researchers keep entering subjects who meet specified criteria into the trial until statistical tests or 'power calculations' indicate that the numbers are sufficient to ensure that observed differences between the trial and control groups are unlikely to be a product of chance. In surveys participants are recruited because they represent in some way a larger group of similar individuals or entities. Therefore central to the survey is the nature of these larger groups and the specific process by which individuals are selected or sampled to represent them. Sampling is designed to minimise the cost of data collection, increase the precision of the data collected (Miller, 2003a, p. 268) and provide evidence on how far the data identified from the samples can be generalised.

The starting point for the selection or sampling process in surveys is the type of information required and the definition of the population about which the researcher wishes to obtain such information. Following on from this are specific strategies for identifying representative individuals or entities from this population through techniques such as random sampling (see for example Miller, 2003a, pp. 268–73). While the researchers try to get all the selected individuals of cases to participate in their research, the reality is that some will not want to participate, so after the recruiting phase the researcher needs to assess how and in what ways this non-response has affected representativeness.

The Expenditure and Food Survey, which uses diaries to monitor expenditure patterns of both adults and children aged 7 to 15, provides a good example of the ways in which participants are recruited for a large-scale diary survey. It is based on two ongoing surveys, one in Great Britain and the other in Northern Ireland. The Office of National Statistics, a government statistical agency in the United Kingdom, organises the survey. The government and other bodies use information from the survey to identify changing patterns of expenditure across the UK (Craggs, 2003, p. 166). The survey uses the household rather than the individual as its basic unit and defines a household as a 'group of people living at the same address with common housekeeping (2003, p. 162). In

Northern Ireland the survey uses addresses on the Valuation and Land Agency list and in Great Britain the 'Small Users file of the Postcode Address File – the Post Office's list of addresses' (2003, p. 162). Sampling in Northern Ireland is straightforward – a random sample of addresses on the list. In Great Britain, the list is stratified in terms of geographic and key social variables and then postal sectors are randomly selected from within these strata (2003, p. 162). The final stage in the process is to check the impact of non-response on the representativeness of the sample which is performed statistically.

The Expenditure and Food Survey deals with the general population aggregated as households; there is a definable population sampling frame, and accessing selected units from this frame is relatively straightforward. When the research involves hard-to-reach groups, for example those that are deprived or socially stigmatised, or elites who protect their privacy (Atkinson and Flint, 2003, p. 275), there is generally no population sampling frame and individuals or groups often prefer to avoid contact.

Generally such groups have to be accessed via an intermediary – an individual or organisation that can provide access and vouch for the research and researcher. Since completing a diary involves a rather longer-term relationship than completing a questionnaire or participating in a one-off interview, such endorsement is particularly important. One possible method of recruitment is to use individuals or institutions that have an established standing within a group or community. For example, migrant groups often have their own language newspapers that can be used to advertise for participants. One problem with this approach is that the researcher has little control over who responds and therefore needs to check the representativeness and likely bias in the response. An alternative which provides more control over the selection of participants is to start with visible and accessible members of the group and, having gained their trust and confidence, use them to identify and access the less visible or 'submerged fraction' of the group (Coxon, 1996, p. 18). Such snowball sampling (also known as chain referral sampling, Biernicki and Wald, 1981) depends on and utilises the social networks that exist within hidden populations (Coxon, 1996, p. 18; Atkinson and Flint, 2003, p. 275). While the researcher has some control over the recruitment process, there is still a problem of bias and the need to check representativeness.

One major diary study of a hard-to-reach group was Project SIGMA, which focused on the sexual activities of men who have sex with men to monitor changes, especially those relevant to HIV transmission (Coxon, 1996, p. vii). The overall project included a number of linked studies between 1987 and 1994 (1996, p. 12) and formed:

> the largest and most detailed longitudinal study of gay and bisexual men and AIDS in Europe and the only study in the UK to have emerged from the gay community itself. (1996, p. vii)

The study started with a critique of existing studies of sexual behaviour of gay men which generally used sexually transmitted disease clinics as their sampling frame. Coxon noted that such populations tended to 'over-represent the younger, more sexually active proportion of the gay population' (1996, p. 3). The notional population for Project SIGMA was 'sexually active men who have sex with men' (1996, p. 17). This avoided the problem of using self-definition of sexual orientation such as 'homosexual' which might both include sexually inactive men and exclude some men who have sex with both men and women. Coxon noted that it was not possible to have an extensive definition of such a population, i.e. one which would define and capture all individuals who formed part of the population, as 'issues of lying and "masking" would introduce enormous biasing factors' (1996, p. 17), and therefore it was not possible to have a population sampling frame.

The Project SIGMA researchers used a number of strategies to access this hard-to-reach population. As gay men, they were able to use the gay press to appeal for volunteers. In November–December 1992 they used *Boyz*, *Pink Paper*, *Capital Gay* (weeklies) and *Gay Times* (monthly) and this produced 79 usable diaries (1996, p. 29). In a later part of the study, Coxon also used snow-ball sampling to recruit diarists in Cardiff and London. To try to achieve representativeness in the sampling he started with a classification of the target group. This was based on age and type of relationship. He identified three age groups:

- men under 21 (for whom sex with other men was illegal)
- men between 21 and 39
- men over 39 (who had grown to maturity before the 1967 Sexual Offences Act when sex with other men was illegal)

and three classes of relationship:

- closed (or monogamous)
- open (with one regular and other partners)
- no regular partner (1996, pp. 17–18).

The research team started recruiting by 'nobbling' the easily accessible part of the populations through gay pubs, clubs and voluntary organisations. They then asked these initial contacts to identify and recruit other potential participants who were similar to them in age and relationship though preferably harder to reach, i.e. less 'out' as gay.

In his 1996 report, Coxon analysed the representativeness of the diarists recruited to the three phases of the project. The sample was biased towards the middle age group (21–39 years), especially for men in an open or no regular relationship (1996, pp. 28–9). The team found it difficult to reach certain types of individuals. Since the recruitment process was anonymous, it was not clear who had nominated second- and third-wave recruits. The chain tended to break down after three links, and weakness in the links probably resulted in the underrepresentation of men who only occasionally engaged in sex with other men (1996, p. 19).

Box 3.2 Key issues researchers should consider when recruiting diarists to participate in a social survey

Purpose of the study

- Is the purpose clearly defined?
- What sort of data is required?
- Which population can supply these data?

Population

- Is the population easy to define and identify?
- Is there an accessible population sampling frame?
- Is the population difficult to define?
- Is the population difficult to access?

Sampling strategies

- Does the population need to be stratified?
- Is it possible to use random sampling of the whole population or defined strata of the population?
- If the population is difficult to define or access, what alternative strategies are available to obtain a sample?

Influence of non-responses

- What is the level of non-response or refusal to participate?
- Is there information on the population that can be used to assess the representativeness of the sample?

Comment

In both experimental and survey research, diaries are a way of accessing knowledge about individuals or cases with specific characteristics. In both styles of research, diarists act as the medium through which the researcher can access this type of knowledge, and therefore recruiting the 'right' diarists is an important part of the research. Diarists must have the competence to maintain a diary. Diarists also have to be 'representative' of a broader population so that the findings of the research can be generalised from the sample to the broader population. In both experimental and survey research, potential participants have to meet specified criteria and there is a systematic mechanism of recruitment designed to avoid bias. This method involves the use of random processes to minimise selection bias. In experiments participants may be randomly allocated to the intervention or control group, while in surveys participants can be randomly selected from a population sampling frame. However it is possible that refusals or non-responses will undermine this process and introduce a systematic bias, and it is necessary to examine the characteristics of the actual participants to identify and allow for any bias.

Engaging diarists in naturalist research

Naturalist researchers approach the recruitment of participants from a different angle. Rather than viewing participants in their research as a means to an end, a way of accessing knowledge about a broader group of cases, naturalistic researchers see the participants in their research as the prime focus and centre of interest. They are curious about how and why this group of individuals act and behave in the way they do. This shift in focus occurred in the ethnographic study of other cultures in the early twentieth century and in sociological studies that focused on personal and community case studies, especially those associated with the Chicago School in the 1920s. Becker described the researcher's role in this approach in the following way:

> he pursues the job from his own perspective, a perspective which emphasizes the value of the person's 'own story'. This perspective differs from that of some other social scientists in assigning major importance to the interpretation people place on their experience as an explanation for behaviour. To understand why someone behaves as he does you must understand how it looked to him; what he thought he had to contend with, what alternatives he saw open to him; you can understand the effects of opportunity structures, delinquent subcultures, social norms, and other commonly invoked explanations of behaviour only by seeing them from the actor's point of view. (2002, p. 80)

Thus a person's story is valued in its own right, not just as a representative sample of a wider category. Researchers using this approach also use systematic strategies to identify potential participants in the research, but rather than starting with the definition of the population from which the sample will be taken and then pursuing systematic sampling strategies to minimise bias, they often begin with the social setting or context within which social interaction and interpretation are taking place. Williams has described two forms of sampling that focus on such characteristics:

> [One approach is] a sample designed to provide a detailed, close-up or meticulous view of cases. The case, or unit, here may be a single individual, location, language, document, conversation etc. [Another] type of sample is that based upon a relevant range of units, related to a 'wider universe', but not representing it directly. The range referred to here might incorporate a range of experiences, characteristics, processes, types, categories, cases of examples, and so on. (2002, p. 132)

As Hammersley and Atkinson (1995, p. 25) note, naturalistic research is often linked to an inductive rather than a deductive approach to research, i.e. the researcher is seeking to generate theories rather than test them. The initial sample may be relatively arbitrary and related to practicalities such as ease of access or convenience as it is the starting point for further selection of cases (1995, pp. 38–9). The findings derived from the initial cases influence the selection and recruitment of subsequent cases. This approach has been systematised within grounded theory as theoretical sampling:

> As we grounded theorists refine our categories and develop them as theoretical con-
> structs, we likely find gaps in our data and holes in our theories. Then we go back to the
> field and collect delimited data to fill those conceptual gaps and holes – we conduct the-
> oretical sampling. At this point, we choose to sample specific issues only; we look for pre-
> cise information to shed light on the emerging theory. Theoretical sampling represents a
> defining property of grounded theory and relies on the comparative methods within
> grounded theory. We use theoretical sampling to develop our emerging categories and
> to make them more definitive and useful. Thus the aim of this sampling is to refine *ideas,*
> not to increase the size of the original sample. Theoretical sampling helps us to identify
> conceptual boundaries and pinpoint the fit and relevance of our categories. (italics in the
> original: Charmaz, 2003, p. 265)

One of the major studies generated by the Chicago School was a study of the migration of Polish peasants to the United States, especially Chicago. The study is based on a collection of documents especially family letters written by Polish peasants during the early twentieth century. While the precise way in which the documents were accessed is not clear, it appears that the researchers started with connections with the local Polish community and accessed documents from a number of families and then expanded their study to include other sources in Poland. As Thomas and Znaniecki (1958a) note, the existence of extensive family correspondence was fairly remarkable, as in the peasant com-munity literacy skills were not highly developed. The letters were the product of a social duty and written by or to an absent family member, including those who had migrated to the United States. There did not appear to have been a tradition of diary keeping in this community, but a major part of the published report is a diary-like autobiography which chronicles in detail the life of Wladek Wiszniewski (Thomas and Znaniecki, 1958b, pp. 1907–13).

Meth (2003) has published an account of the ways diarists were recruited to a study in South Africa which was designed to explore women's experience and fear of violence. The study focused on one category of women, poor black women, and recruited from three locations in Durban. The recruitment was a two-stage process. Initially women were invited to participate in focus groups and then focus group participants were invited to take part in the diary study. Facilitators in each locality undertook the initial recruitment of 40 women for the group interviews using their networks and local organisations such as churches. At the end of each group the participants were invited to take part in the diary study and all agreed. The sessions were also used to explain the aims of the diary study and researchers' expectations and to answer questions.

In some ways the exercise worked well. Thirty-nine of the participants returned diaries. However there were some difficulties and some of the documents did not meet the strict criteria for a diary, i.e. that it should be a personal, contemporaneous record. The researchers had not assessed diarists' competence or understanding of the conventions of diary keeping. They wanted the diarists to write their entries in Zulu and it was clear at the initial induction that a number were not literate in Zulu. The researchers agreed that the diarists could use a surrogate to write their entries, a school-going child or someone they trusted. The diaries were intended to explore sensitive issues such as violence within the household, yet this meant that some diaries were filtered through a third party.

Jones and his colleagues (2000) in Hong Kong undertook a diary and questionnaire study of a hard-to-reach population, tongji or men who have sex with men. The diary part of their study was designed to capture the experiences plus related attitudes, feelings and beliefs of men who have sex with men to:

> establish the core issues, concerns and practices of the target population and to generate theories about the ways these issues, concerns, and practices affect members likelihood to engage in high risk behaviour. (2000, p. 8)

The follow-up questionnaire survey was designed to test out the validity of these findings on a larger sample of the population. The research team used 'purposive sampling', deliberately and non-randomly selecting from different age groups and backgrounds ethnic Chinese, Cantonese speaking men who have sex with men. They used a variety of sources to recruit such as contacts in tongji organisations, an ad in a gay magazine and personal contacts. The team used an initial telephone interview to screen potential participants for suitability and invited 18 suitable participants to attend an initial orientation session. The team successfully obtained 16 diaries from which they identified 49 narratives of sexual behaviour. The diarists came from a variety of backgrounds.

Comment

While researchers using experimental and survey designs emphasise the importance of rigorous and systematic approaches to identifying suitable diarists and the need to check the characteristics of the actual sample recruited to identify potential bias, researchers engaged in naturalistic designs are more relaxed and pragmatic about their initial starting point. Naturalistic researchers are often interested in generating rather than testing hypotheses and theories so that initial openness to ideas and possibilities is important and initial ideas can be tested out in subsequent more systemic selection of participants as in theoretical sampling. Naturalistic research is based on respect for the participants in the research (Hammersley and Atkinson, 1995, p. 6) so each participant and his or her account is valued. Whereas a single account would be treated as unrepresentative in experimental or survey work, in naturalistic research a single account can become a 'life history' which can be used as a case study to generate insights and understanding into a specific phenomenon.

Box 3.3 Key issues researchers should consider when recruiting diarists to participate in a naturalistic study

Purpose of the study

- Is the purpose clearly defined?
- What sort of data is required?
- Which groups and individuals should the researcher seek to engage?

Building up relationships and contact

- Is there an initial point of contact?
- How can further contact with the target individuals be made?

Building up trust

- Is the researcher acceptable to the group?
- To what extent will the researcher's presence disrupt natural relations and activities?
- How can the researcher build up relationships and persuade members of the group to keep personal records of activities?

Accessing unsolicited diaries

In the previous two sections, I examined the ways in which researchers could solicit diaries for research. Since diaries are personal documents, this discussion focused on the methods by which researchers identify suitable participants, that is individuals with the suitable skills and commitment to provide appropriate information and data. In this section I will consider the ways in which researchers can find and access unsolicited diaries. Since these documents predate the researchers' interest in them, the main issues relate to the likely location of relevant diaries and method of access. Broadly I differentiate between recent diaries that are still in the possession of the diarist or their immediate family and friends, and historical diaries that have been placed or are stored in some form of archive of historical documents. The difference between the two forms of diary relates more to access than to time. For example Samuel Pepys on his death donated his library including his diary to Magdalene College Cambridge where they were accessible to scholars (Tomalin, 2002, pp. 374–5); while the original diaries of Ralph Josselin, who was a contemporary of Pepys, were still in private ownership in the 1960s though a partial version had been published in 1908 (Hockliffe, 1908) and a complete microfilm and transcript had been deposited in the Essex County Records Office (MacFarlane, 1970, p. 10). I will first consider accessing recent or contemporary diaries and then historical diaries.

Diaries in private possession

Most recent diaries remain in the private possession of the diarist or their immediate family or friends and therefore there is no formal record of their existence or public mechanism of access. Thus accessing such documents involves strategies to identify individuals who may have and control access to diaries. The researcher can seek to identify potential diary holders but this is likely to be a time consuming exercise as only a small proportion of the target group is likely to hold diaries. It is likely to be more cost effective to use an intermediary that has contact with potential diary holders. The media have proved very effective at generating and capturing narratives of the recent past including diaries. Media interest in the Second World War, for example, grew in the United Kingdom with a succession of 60th anniversaries of key events such as the D-Day landings. The British Broadcasting Corporation actively promotes and manages an internet archive of personal stories of the war. While these accounts have to be transcribed and submitted electronically they constitute a rapidly growing archive of personal documents. The BBC described the purpose of the archive in the following way:

> Everyone has a story to tell. Share your World War Two memories.
>
> WW2 People's War is a site dedicated to capturing people's personal stories of World War Two in a lasting archive. Whether the writer was military or civilian, at home or abroad, on the front-line or home front, every story plays a vital part in helping future generations understand the sacrifices made by a nation at war.
>
> If you lived through the war, please contribute your story; you can now add pictures too. Or if you know someone who remembers those days but is not used to computers, why not help them add their account? For a full explanation of how to make contributions to the site – take the Guided Tour [link].
>
> Please note that WW2 People's War is an internet-only project, which means that contributions made by letter or telephone cannot be accepted. However, there are now over 2,000 People's War centres nationwide where you can find help getting your story online. If you would like information about your nearest People's War centre, please call the helpline on 08000 150950. (WW2 People's War Team, 2004)

There are few published accounts of the ways in which researchers have accessed privately held diaries. Miller (1985) in his study of Irish migrants in the United States followed Thomas and Znaniecki's (1958a) example and used unsolicited personal documents, mostly letters but also some diaries. In the appendix he listed the privately held documents which he accessed between 1972 and 1983. From the acknowledgements it is clear that Miller used institutions and individuals with contacts in the Irish migrant community to access documents held in private hands, including a former US ambassador to

Ireland, the American Irish Foundation and the Immigration Sources Project at the University of Michigan.

Archived diaries

When documents such as diaries are placed in archives they acquire the status of historical documents, i.e. are seen as having intrinsic value because of their age or the status of the person who kept them. Increasingly, personal documents including those solicited during research are being archived. The ESRC Data Archive at the University of Essex initially focused on quantitative data, especially from surveys. The Archive has now established Qualidata and an Economic and Social Data Service to encourage researchers to archive data and to improve researchers' access to qualitative data such as diaries (Corti et al., 2003, p. 244). When I searched the Qualidata website using 'diary' as a keyword, I identified 144 entries (ESDA Qualidata, 2005). Most of these were diaries which had been collected as part of large-scale and well-known UK surveys such as the Expenditure and Food Surveys and Project SIGMA.

Given the relative paucity of diary data held within such dedicated data archives, researchers who want to access unsolicited diaries still have to rely on archives of historical documents. Generally diaries only form a small part of a wider archive and accessing in particular involves developing knowledge of potential archives and their contents. This means that sources which provide a general catalogue of archives are not particularly helpful (see for example Foster and Sheppard, 1995). There are, however, a number of sources that focus specifically on archived or published diaries. Matthews has published a bibliography of American diaries (1945) and British diaries (1950). Since then Arksey (1983; 1986) has published two volumes on American diaries and Havlice (1987) has published one on all diaries published in English. Increasingly such printed compilations are being supplemented or replaced by electronic versions which can be accessed via the internet. For example the Penn Library (2004) has produced a research guide to finding diaries using its own catalogue system and two others in the US.

There are some archived diaries which can be accessed through online data sources. The Mass Observation archive is particularly valuable because of its collection of diary materials. Mass Observation was a social research organisation founded to develop an 'anthropology of ourselves' which 'invited members of the public to record their day-to-day lives in the form of a diary' (Sheridan, 1991, p. 1). Mass Observation recruited 500 men and women, most of whom kept a diary from 1939 until 1945 and some continued until 1965. These diaries remained in a London basement until 1970 when the University of Sussex created an archive for all the Mass Observation papers. The archive maintains a website that provides information both on the diaries archived and on publications based on the diaries (for an index to archived diaries see http://www.sussex.ac.uk/library/massobs/diaries_1939-65.html).

Pollock's (1983) use of diaries to study childhood and especially the ways in which parents actually reared their children is a well-developed example of the use of unsolicited diaries in social research. Pollock wanted to find out how rearing patterns changed over time (1500–1900) and used personal documents such as diaries and autobiographies as they provided insight into actual child rearing at specific times rather than expert opinion on how children should be raised which formed the basis of published child rearing guides. She started her search for diaries that contained accounts of child rearing using the standard bibliographic sources available at the time, especially Matthew's bibliographies of American (1945) and British diaries (1950), and used the National Bibliography catalogue to identify post-1950 diaries (Pollock, 1983, p. 69). In addition she identified Ralph Josselin's diary from MacFarlane's (1970) study and another eight diaries by looking through the British Library catalogue. In total she identified 416 usable documents, including 114 American diaries, 236 British diaries and 36 autobiographies. Ninety-eight of the diaries were written by children or started when the diarist was a child (Pollock, 1983, p. 69).

Comment

Researchers who use unsolicited diaries for their research have to identify where suitable diaries are likely to be held. Recent diaries are likely to be held privately by diarists or their immediate family and therefore the researcher needs to locate potential diary holders through his or her personal contacts or via an intermediary such as a trusted agency or the media. Historical diaries are held in archives and therefore the researcher needs to identify target archives and explore their contents, possibly aided by bibliographic sources.

Box 3.4 Key issues researchers should consider when accessing unsolicited diaries

What sort of diaries

- What sort of diaries are likely to provide the information needed for the research?
- Are the diaries recent, historical or a mixture?

Recent diaries

- What groups are likely to hold diaries?
- What are the most effective ways of making contact with possible diary holders?

Historical diaries

- Can these be identified from existing bibliographies?
- If yes, what additional sources should be used?
- If no, which archives are likely to hold relevant diaries?

Summary and comment

Having decided on the aims of the research, the researcher needs to identify the source of data. For solicited diaries this will involve identifying suitable diarists, and definitions of suitability will be made in terms of the purposes of the research, its specific design, the target population or group and the skills which the diarist needs to effectively maintain his or her diary. For unsolicited diaries the researcher will need to identify where such diaries are likely to be held and how they can be accessed.

KEY POINTS

Overall

- The purpose and design of the research will influence the choice of diaries.

Experimental and survey research

- Given the importance of generalisation of the findings, it is necessary to start by defining the population.
- If all individuals or entities in the population can be identified and listed, i.e. a population sampling frame exists, then the researcher should use an explicit and systematic strategy to identify potential diarists.
- If it is not possible to identify or access a sampling frame, then the researcher needs to use a pragmatic approach to recruitment such as snowballing.

Soliciting diaries for naturalistic research

- Initially participants or cases may be selected on relatively pragmatic grounds, as analysis of initial accounts will generate insights and influence selection of subsequent settings and participants, e.g. using theoretical sampling.
- Each account will be treated as a valuable source and a single diary can be used as a critical case study and form the basis of a 'life history'.

Unsolicited diaries

- The researcher must identify what sort of diaries are likely to be suitable for the research and where such diaries are likely to be held.
- Recent diaries are likely to be held by diarists or their immediate family or friends. The researcher has to find a way of reaching potential diary holders through advertising or through an intermediary.

- Historical diaries are likely to be held in archives though some will also be published. The researcher will need to identify potential archives and use available bibliographic sources.

EXERCISE

This exercise provides scenarios for three different research projects. For each you are invited to consider how you would identify suitable diarists or diaries.

Project 1

The Department for Education and Skills is concerned about the work stress among teachers in primary and secondary schools and wants to find out whether disruptive pupils and changes in level of required documentation are affecting the ways in which teachers manage their time. The DfES has commissioned a diary-based study, and has agreed to provide access to a national register of qualified teachers, which includes age, type of qualification, current employment and location of employment. Develop a strategy for selecting participants for the study.

Project 2

A consortium of health agencies is reviewing the services for older people who have had a stroke in their area. The agencies have access to data on the costs and throughput of current services but want to take into account the patients' experience of treatment and care, especially longer-term rehabilitation and support in the community, and want a longitudinal diary study. Stroke survivors have very different pathways: some are admitted to stroke units and others to general medical wards, and some do not even go into hospital. How will you recruit participants to your study?

Project 3

You are considering applying to the Economic and Social Research Council for funding of a historical study to explore the hypothesis that the modern epidemic of drug misuse reflects a shift from the early modern period in which a narrow range of psychoactive substances were used in a socially sanctioned and controlled fashion to the current situation of experimentation with and access to a wide range of psychoactive substances. Outline how you would identify and access suitable diaries for your study.

4

Collecting the Data: Diaries, Guidelines and Support

When carefully managed, and with suitable co-operation from informants, the diary can be used to record data that might not be forthcoming in face-to-face interviews or other data collection encounters. (Hammersley and Atkinson, 1995, p. 164)

Key aims
- To examine how researchers can carefully manage research diaries to ensure the suitable co-operation of diarists.

Key objectives
- To examine the alternative ways in which researchers can structure diaries to generate material that is suitable for their research.
- To examine the ways in which researchers can build up and maintain a relationship with diarists.
- To examine the type of instructions and/or guidelines which researchers can provide for diarists.

Structuring diaries

Researchers differ in the degree to which they want to control the type of information which diarists record. Researchers using experimental and survey designs want diarists to record only data which are relevant to the research and to record them in a highly structured way. They will seek to rigidly structure the documents used by diarists and provide detailed instructions and training to ensure that diarists use the documents supplied correctly. Researchers using unsolicited diaries have by definition no control over the ways in which these diaries were created. They have to use what is available and select diaries which contain relevant information. Researchers soliciting diaries for naturalistic research do have the opportunity to influence the ways in which diarists keep their diaries but for such researchers there is a tension. While they want diarists to be free to produce their own accounts in their own words, they may want to provide some guidance so that diarists address relevant issues.

Researchers using experimental designs often emphasise their role as a neutral independent observer 'who systematically observes and measures the behaviour of matter' and reports the results of these investigations as facts (Bowling, 2002, p. 126). Thus there is a strong emphasis on ensuring the observations and measurements are accurate and not subject to bias. In this approach to research, 'diaries are a substitute for accurate scientific observation, in settings from which the "scientist" is absent' (Elliott, 1997, p. 3). Participants will undermine the research if they do not accurately measure and record the effects of the prescribed interventions (Ross et al., 2001, p. 44). Survey researchers are also concerned with accuracy. Vagueness of instruction or misunderstandings about the information which the diarist should record can produce inaccuracies in the data recorded in diaries (McColl et al., 2001, pp. 253–4).

Researchers using qualitative and naturalistic approaches to research are more concerned with the authenticity of participants' accounts. They want to use methods which show respect for participants and minimise intrusion into their social worlds (Hammersley and Atkinson, 1995, p. 6). Researchers using unsolicited diaries are in an excellent position to adopt a naturalistic approach, while researchers soliciting diaries need to consider the impact which their soliciting has on the research setting.

Unsolicited diaries can be treated as documents which represent naturalistic life stories. Such stories form part of a person's everyday life and are not structured or prompted by the researcher:

> Naturalistic life stories are not artificially assembled but just happen *in situ*. They tell it as it is: with such voices there is a natural fidelity to the world as the life story tellers find it. (italics in the original: Plummer, 2001, p. 27)

Diary keepers develop such naturalistic documents as 'day to day [they] strive to record an ever-changing present' (2001, p. 48). Researchers soliciting diaries inevitably intrude into the natural setting and, like all solicited materials, diaries have to be 'coaxed' out of subjects (2001, p. 27). Researchers need to decide how and in what ways they will structure the diary keeping and use diary keeping. They will need to explain the purpose of diary keeping and the diaries and persuade individuals, many of whom are not in the habit of diary keeping, to keep one especially for the research. They may need to provide the means of keeping a diary and to give guidance on the ways in which they would like the diarist to keep their diary.

Structuring diaries in experimental and social surveys

Researchers using diaries for experimental and survey research can control the data collection process in a number of ways, by providing: a highly structured method of recording data; a detailed set of instructions for diarists on how they should use the diary recording system; training in maintaining the diary; and a mechanism for checking the accuracy of the records.

Structuring the record keeping system

While all diaries have some degree of structure, they involve regular entries; diaries used for experimental or social surveys need a more formal structure to ensure that relevant data are recorded. The more precise and clearly defined the research question or hypothesis, the easier it is to specify precisely the type of data required and the appropriate design of the diary recording system. Each project will need to develop its own unique diary structure, and to develop the optimum structure the research may need to try out or pilot several versions. However such diaries are likely to have common features. The diary will usually take the form of a series of printed or electronic sheets. Each sheet will have a space for entering the date and if appropriate the precise time when the record was made, and a space or mechanism for making the necessary record. Corti provides a helpful set of guidelines for structuring a paper diary:

- An A4 booklet of about 5 to 20 pages is desirable, depending on the nature of the diary.
- Depending on how long a period the diary will cover, each page denoting either a week, a day of the week or a 24 hour period or less. Pages should be clearly ruled up as a calendar with prominent headings and enough space to enter all the desired information (such as what the respondent was doing, at what time, where, who with and how they felt at the time, and so on).
- Appropriate terminology or lists of activities should be designed to meet the needs of the sample under study, and if necessary, different versions of the diary should be used for different groups.
- Following the diary pages it is useful to include a simple set of questions for the respondent to complete, asking, among other things, whether the diary keeping period was atypical in any way compared to usual daily life. It is also good practice to include a page at the end asking for the respondents' own comments and clarifications of any peculiarities relating to their entries. Even if these remarks will not be systematically analysed, they may prove helpful at the editing or coding stage. (1993, pp. 2–3)

Parkin and his colleagues (2004) used Corti's guidelines to develop the diaries for their study of the effects of beta interferon therapy on 62 people with relapsing-remitting multiple sclerosis over a six-week period. The diaries took the form of spiral-bound booklets with pages colour coded to differentiate between weeks. The diary was clearly structured into weeks and individuals days, and for each day there was a series of questions:

> For each daily entry, they [diarists] were asked to indicate whether they had experienced any of a list of symptoms for the day, if so, how much of a problem each had been and to what extent it had interfered with what they wanted to do; what they had done; how good or bad their health had been (using the EQ VAS), whether it had been better, worse or about the same as usual; and whether or not they needed help completing the diary entry. (2004, p. 353)

The diarists were invited to assess their health by entering a measurement on a printed design, the EQ VAS which had a 'thermometer' design.

Guidance on using diaries

Researchers using complex recording systems cannot assume that diarists will know how to maintain their diaries and therefore need to provide advice, guidance or instructions for diarists. Again Corti (1993) provides helpful guidelines on the provision of guidance. She suggests that guidance can be built into the structure of each diary in a number of ways:

- The inside cover page should contain a clear set of instructions on how to complete the diary. This should stress the importance of recording events as soon as possible after they occur and how the respondent should try not to let the diary keeping influence their behaviour.
- A model example of a correctly completed diary should feature on the second page.
- Checklists of the items, events or behaviour to help jog the diary keeper's memory should be printed somewhere fairly prominent. Very long lists should be avoided since they may be off-putting and confusing to respondents. For a structured time budget diary, an exhaustive list of all possible relevant activities should be listed together with the appropriate codes. Where more than one type of activity is to be entered, that is, primary and secondary (or background) activities, guidance should be given on how to deal with 'competing' or multiple activities.
- There should be an explanation of what is meant by the unit of observation, such as a 'session', an 'event' or a 'fixed time block'. Where respondents are given more freedom in naming their activities and the activities are to be coded later, it is important to give strict guidelines on what type of behaviour to include, what definitely to exclude and the level of detail required. Time budget diaries without fixed time blocks should include columns for start and finish times for activities. (1993, pp. 2–3)

Coxon (1996) in his account of the use of sexual diaries provided a detailed description of the guidance which his team provided for diarists. The diary used open text as the team could not specify in advance the number, frequency and nature of sexual sessions which any specific diarist would engage in. The basic structure of the diaries was simple: four sheets, one per week, with seven open text boxes (days) on each sheet (1996, p. 176). To ensure that diarists wrote the entries in an appropriate format, the team provided detailed guidance and instructions for diary entries. Each diary sheet contained a summary of the guidance:

> Remember, each session should include:
>> The Time, The Place, The Partners (from the partner list).
>> Then, describe the session in your own words.
>
> Remember to mention exactly what happened to the 'come' (ejaculate) and always mention the use of condoms.
>
> List any accompaniments you use (poppers, lubricants, drugs, sex toys ...).
> Mention how much you drank each day if it is associated with sex.
>
> **If a diary entry is too small, carry on overleaf, or add a page (remembering to identify the time, day and date).** (bold in the original: 1996, p. 176)

The diary also contained a full set of instructions that specified in more detail how the diary should be used. Most of these instructions were concerned with ensuring the diaries were an accurate record of sexual sessions and specified in detail how such sessions and the sexual acts they contained should be recorded. There was also more generic guidance on the way to keep the diary, stressing the importance of honesty and accuracy:

> Please read these notes carefully before you start recording your sexual diary.
> In your diary we would like you to keep a full, detailed record of your sexual activities.
>
> **Put each entry in as soon as possible after it occurs,** preferably on the day it happens.
> **Please be completely honest** when recording your diary, otherwise it isn't worth filling in. For instance, if you aren't having much sex at the moment, please don't invent activity, or if you didn't use a condom don't say you did! From our point of view a diary with little in it is as significant as a full one.
> **Please write as clearly as you can.** If you can't fit everything into an entry, continue on the back of the sheet or on a separate sheet, remembering to mark the date on which the entry occurred.
> You may feel that some times are unlike your usual sexual behaviour (e.g. holidays); please keep writing, though – this is all important information.
> If you decide you don't want to do a diary, or find you can't complete the full month, *please return the brief questionnaire at the beginning of the diary, and whatever part you have completed.*
> Although we are mainly concerned with sex with other men, please make sure you record any sex you have with women during the diary period. (bold and italic in the original: 1996, p. 176)

Training and checking the accuracy of diaries

Structuring the diaries and including written instructions are relatively impersonal ways of influencing diarists. They can be supplemented by more personal approaches, including training and feedback on initial entries.

Training usually involves face-to-face sessions with individual or groups of diarists in which a representative of the research teams explains the purpose of the study, the role of diary keeping within the study and the way in which diarists should maintain their diaries, and answers any questions. Parkin and his colleagues (2004) included a training session in their beta interferon therapy for people who have relapsing-remitting multiple sclerosis. A few days after participants in the study had completed an initial questionnaire, a member of the research team visited them and showed them how to complete a model entry (2004, p. 353). Such training is probably most effective but is also time consuming. In our own diary study of nurses and risk (Alaszewski et al., 2000) we allowed a day for the first visit including travel time, a briefing interview plus guidance on how to complete the diary.

It is important that the researchers maintain contact with diarists and obtain feedback so that problems can be quickly identified. It is often helpful if the first few diary entries are treated as a pilot for learning purposes before the diarist enters the study proper, so that the researchers can identify any problems and provide additional guidance on diary entries. Hyland et al. (1993) suggested that such diaries could provide an important source of data if due allowance was made for error. Their review showed that the quality of diary completion was often poor. However they argued that rather than blaming diarists for poor record keeping, it was important that researchers recognised that their expectations might be unreasonable and that diarists, like all humans, were liable to forget. It would make more sense to design studies that accommodate human forgetfulness and error and, in particular, provide instructions that tell the patient what to do when a day is missed. Coupled with such instructions, electronic, time coded diaries provided a more effective way of ensuring the quality of diary records (1993, pp. 488-9).

Comment

Researchers using diaries for experimental and survey research are concerned with the accuracy of the data recorded. There are a number of strategies which they can use to enhance the quality of the data. They can design diaries which are user-friendly. Such diaries should include simple instructions which clearly specify how the diarists should record relevant information. If the type of data required can clearly be specified in advance then the researchers should consider how they can structure each unit of data collection, whether this is a day or a specific event, using limited choice or closed questions modelled on those used in questionnaires.

Box 4.1 Key issues the researcher should consider when designing a diary for use in experimental or survey research

Diary structure

- What sort of data do you want to collect?
- Can these data be collected through structured instruments?
- If so, are there designs from other studies to use as a guide for the design of your diary?
- If you design your own structured instrument, how will you pilot it?
- If you use structured instruments, what will be the balance between structured instruments and free text space?

Instructions

- What overall instructions should be given at the start of the diary on completion, missed entries, returning diaries and contact with researchers?
- What instructions should be provided on each sheet in relationship to: structured data collection instruments; and free text?
- How can you check that the instructions are comprehensible for the target population?

Contact with diarists

- How will the diary be given to the diarist?
- When and where can training be provided?
- Is there a mechanism for answering diarists' queries?
- Is there a mechanism for providing ongoing support such as a contact phone number or email address?

Checking the quality of data

- Can the data be checked?
- Is it possible to check a sample entry at an early stage?
- What sort of feedback will be provided?

Naturalistic research and diaries

Naturalistic researchers are interested in accessing knowledge about social realities that is not contaminated by the research process. As I noted in the first section in this chapter, unsolicited diaries come close to this ideal. However given the selective nature of both diary keeping and the survival of diaries, they tend to provide better records for groups among whom diary keeping is a well-established habit: historically literate elites. Since researchers using unsolicited diaries cannot influence the type of entries which the diarists chose to make in their diaries, they have to decide which diaries are appropriate for the purpose of their research. MacFarlane, who wanted an insight into the 'mental life of people who lived long ago' (1970, p. 3), found an ideal source in the very detailed diaries which Ralph Josselin, a rural vicar in Essex, kept from 1644 until his death in 1683.

Issues in using solicited diaries

Researchers using solicited diaries face something of a dilemma. They want diaries to record what diarists see as relevant and important and therefore the diary design will tend towards 'an open format, allowing respondents to record activities and events in their own words' (Corti, 1993, p. 2). At the same time they may be interested in a specific aspect of the diarists' experiences. For example Meth (2003) in her study used diaries to access women's experiences in South Africa. While she was interested in the broader context of everyday events, her main interest was in the ways in which women experienced violence in a violent society. Thus she wanted her diarists to focus on issues of violence:

> I encouraged women to write about what they wanted to *in relation to fear, crime and violence.* (italics added: 2003, p. 199)

This dilemma is present in most forms of naturalistic research but often there are ways of managing it. For example, researchers using participant observation have the time and opportunity to build up relationships of confidence and trust so that they can access insiders' views. Researchers using interviews can seek to develop a relationship with their interviewees using their social skills to guide the conversation towards the areas and issues that interest the researchers (Hammersley and Atkinson, 1995, p. 152). In diary research it is more difficult to build up a close relationship and to guide diarists towards areas of interest to the researchers, as diarists choose where, when and how to complete their diaries and the researcher is not present when diarists makes such decisions. Researchers can use several approaches to guide diarists towards issues that are relevant for the purpose of their research. For instance they can make the diary itself user-friendly, provide face-to-face explanations and informal written guidance, and use diaries alongside interviews as part of a diary-interview method.

THE DIARY

The diaries used in experimental and survey studies tend to be purpose designed and produced specifically for the research. In contrast, researchers using diaries for naturalistic research want to emphasise the ordinariness of the process of diary keeping and the extent to which diarists can use their diaries to express themselves. Thus they will either use ready-made commercially available diaries or booklets of lined paper or produce fairly simple ordinary

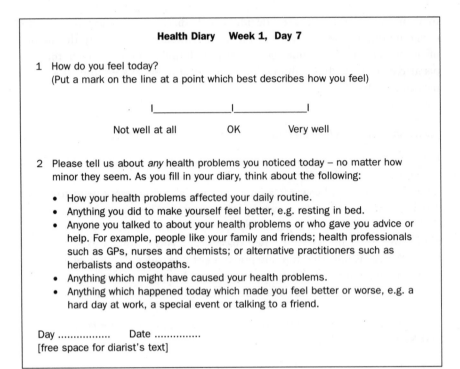

FIGURE 4.1   *Format of Elliott's health diary (Elliott, 1997, para. 3.3)*

looking documents. For example in our own study of the ways in which community nurses managed the risks of their everyday practice (Alaszewski et al., 2000) we purchased small (22.5 cm × 17.5 cm) ring-bound 100-page booklets that had 25 lines per page from a stationery shop. We did not alter the booklets in any way apart from inserting an initial page of guidance. We wanted to enable the diarists to introduce their own structure. Generally diarists used one or two pages per day, completing up to 20 pages of the booklet.

Elliott (1997) created a more formal document for the diarists in her study of the help seeking behaviours of eight people who were aware of having musculoskeletal problems. In addition to a formal first page with the title *Health Diary* and details of who was completing the diary and when, Elliott produced separate sheets for each day (see Figure 4.1).

FACE-TO-FACE CONTACT

Given the emphasis in naturalistic research on the relationship between the researcher and the participants in research, it is important to find and use opportunities to meet and talk to potential diarists both to explain the overall aim of the study and the specific ways in which the researcher wants diarists to use their diaries and to provide participants with an opportunity to express their concerns and ask questions. Meth (2003) and her co-researchers in their study of South African women's experiences of violence initially invited women to participate in focus groups, and then at the end of the group interview invited participants to take part in the diary part of the study and explained how they wanted diarists to keep their diaries. They invited questions and discussions and dealt with practical issues such as 'running out of pages, not being able to return the diary on the specified date and not knowing what to write' (2003, p. 197).

While Meth concentrated on an initial briefing session to build up a relationship with her diarists, researchers can create other opportunities to meet and provide support and guidance to diarists. In our own study of the ways in which community nurses managed risk (Alaszewski et al., 2000, pp. 81–2) we used an initial briefing interview to explain the purposes of the diaries and give the diarists initial guidance. At this meeting we arranged to visit the diarist after he or she had completed one entry so we could review the entry with the diarist and provide any additional guidance or answer any questions.

WRITTEN GUIDANCE

Researchers can also provide written guidance for diarists. It is important that this guidance is not too prescriptive so that diarists are encouraged to write about the issues of interest to the researchers in their own words. Drawing further on our diary study of nurses and risk (Alaszewski et al., 2000), in the pilot study we found that participants tended to identify risk with high consequence incidents. Therefore we encouraged the diarists to write broadly about their activities and decision-making by providing the following statement as part of the guidance on the front inside cover of each diary:

The aim of this phase is to ask a number of practitioner nurses to:

  i.   describe their nursing activities during a normal shift
 ii.   identify two or three decisions which were made in relation to patients
iii.   discuss whether training had prepared them for participation in the decision making. If not, would any additional training have helped?

The practitioner is asked to write 100 to 150 words per shift on the above points.

Elliott (1997) in her study of help seeking patterns provided her diarists with relatively detailed guidelines on how to use their diaries (see Figure 4.2).

While such guidelines are designed to be helpful, diarists may experience them as directive and restrictive. An alternative approach is to provide diarists with exemplars so that they can get a feel for the type of issues the researchers want to explore. In a project designed to explore the ways in which stroke survivors responded to their stroke and developed their lives after their stroke

How to fill in your diary

Thank you for agreeing to help us with our study. Here are some points to bear in mind when filling in your diary.

- We are interested in all your health problems – not just problems associated with arthritis or rheumatism.

- Remember that this is *your* diary. We are interested in finding out as much as possible about your health and your experiences of using health services and other care. So please tell us as much as you can about yourself – no matter how unimportant it seems. For example, if you made an appointment with your GP and then had to cancel it or if you felt under the weather but decided not to do anything about it or if you treated a bad cold yourself by staying in bed with a hot whisky – we'd like to know. If you are not sure whether to tell us about something or not, please include it – we would rather have too much information than too little.

- Please don't worry about spelling, grammar or 'best' handwriting but try to write as clearly as you can, using a pen.

- Try to fill in the diary *every evening*. If you cannot make an entry for a particular day, then you can fill it in the following day. However, do not try to fill the diary in any later than one day after the entry was due – e.g. don't try to fill in Monday's entry on Wednesday.

- If you find that you have missed out several days, please do not give up the whole week's diary. Just start again on the next day you are able to fill it in, and leave the other pages blank.

- Please fill in the day and date in the space provided on each new diary page.

- If you have any questions about the health diary, please phone Heather Elliott on 0161 xxx xxxx. She will phone you back, so you do not have to pay for the call.

FIGURE 4.2   *Elliott's guidelines for her health diary (Elliott, 1997, para. 3.3)*

(Alaszewski and Alaszewski, 2005) we used diaries to capture the ways in which survivors managed their recovery. In addition to providing guidance on the aims and objectives of the diaries we provided exemplars from diaries in a pilot study of the ways in which diarists could use their diaries:

1.   **Please provide a short account of how you spent the day.**

For example, Mr Jones wrote:

7th April Monday
A bright morning although it was a cold wind. My wife went to Marie Louise with some figures to do some accounts with her. While she was away the chap came with the electric wheelchair. As well as fitting a new battery, had put on more heavy duty tyres. My wife took me for a spin up to the cottage. Daughter came and stayed the night and is beginning to feel better.

For example, Mr Neville wrote:

Tuesday 11/02/03

Awoken at 04.50. Listened to World News BBC at 05.00. Switch radio off at 05.40. Listened to bird song, dawn chorus. Rose from bed at 06.40. Prepared tea tray. Did 300 revolutions of pedals on exercise bicycle. Had early morning tea whilst watching the news on TV.

2. How did you feel about today – did anything make you feel particularly pleased or fed up? Did you think it had been a good or a bad day?

For example, Mr Jones wrote:

Felt I got somewhere today … getting back the wheelchair. Getting my daughter back again so well could go out again.

For example, Mr Charles wrote:

During the afternoon I removed and changed the filters in the cooker hood. This was significant as it made me use both my brains and my hands.

3. Did you have any contact with any professionals (physios, nurses etc.) or access any information on stroke (e.g. on TV or in a newspaper)? How did you feel about this contact or information? Was it helpful or not and why?

For example, Mr Jones wrote:

Got up early and waited to see Joanne the Speech and Language Therapist at the Health Centre. We discussed ways on how I can improve my writing and also my telephone conversations.
Most important point today: going to health centre and meeting Joanne. She had some very good ideas to help me improve.

For example, Mr Jones wrote:

Important point: my wife listened to me reading aloud some of the important points in the paper. I realised then that Joanne [the Speech and Language Therapist] had suggested I do this to help my speech.

The diary-interview method

The diary-interview methods (Zimmerman and Wieder, 1977) provide a structure for diary research that links diaries to interviews. This approach has three components: an initial interview, the research diary and the debriefing interview. The initial interview provides participants with a briefing about how they should use their diaries and provides an opportunity for questions about the diary. The participants maintain their diary for a specified period and at an agreed time return them to the research team. The team then read and analyse the diaries and use their analysis as the basis of a debriefing interview. Zimmerman and Wieder developed their approach as an alternative to participant observation in order to access settings and activities which they could not directly observe. They recruited insiders whom they asked to keep detailed diaries for seven-day periods and then they interviewed each diarist. In these interviews each diarist:

was asked not only to expand the reportage, but also was questioned on the less directly observable features of the events recorded, on their meanings, their propriety, typicality, connection with other events and so on. (1977, p. 481)

Elliott (1997) also used this approach. She maintained close contact with the participants in her study, visiting them at least three times: once to brief them and give them their diary; a second time to collect their first diary (this second visit provided an opportunity for an initial 'conversation' about the diary); and a third and final visit to conduct an in-depth interview (1997, p. 4). Elliott used the conversations and interviews to explore themes identified in the interviews. In the interviews, participants revealed not only actions that they took in relationship to their health but also actions they did not take or intended to take at some time in the future. For example in his diary Mr D. recorded an episode of intense pain in his leg but he recorded that he did not tell his wife about it. Elliott (1997, p. 7) noted the value of the follow-up interviews in explaining such actions. She emphasised the ways in which she used the diary-interview process to involve diarists in the research. She observed that in the interviews some diarists referred to their diaries, using them as *aides-mémoire*, and therefore the interviews:

> were grounded in the texts mainly authored by informants and reiterated informants' own terms for describing their experience rather than being based on researchers' texts, such as interview schedules or questionnaires or researchers' terms of reference ... They were collaborators in the construction of the account and had a stake in the research process. (1997, p. 9)

Comment

Researchers using naturalistic approaches want to minimise the disruption and distortions which the research process makes to the social realities they are seeking to examine and understand. Researchers using unsolicited diaries can argue that their research does not influence such realities though they have to deal with the processes associated with the production, survival and storage of such documents. Researchers who solicit diaries as part of the research process may change the behaviour of the people engaged in the research. Diary keeping is a minority habit and therefore most of the participants in a diary study will not usually keep a diary. The researchers will normally seek to minimise the intrusion, creating diaries that are open in structure and informal. The objective is to enhance the diarists' control over the ways in which they use their diaries. Researchers will avoid detailed prescriptive instructions that restrict diarists' freedom of expression. Instead the researcher will seek to influence the diary keeping process by developing a relationship with the diarist through regular contact initiated before the diary period, maintained during the diary keeping period with perhaps visits to look at sample entries or to collect initial diaries, and culminating in a final visit which in the diary-interview method is formalised into a debriefing interview.

Box 4.2 Key issues the researcher should consider when designing a diary for use in naturalistic research

Diary format

- Should the diary contain structured elements or should it be primarily free text?
- If it is primarily free text, is it possible to use a ready-made or commercially produced document?
- If the diary is specially designed and produced for the purposes of the research: how and where will background information be produced; and how will the structured and free text components be balanced?

Guidance

- How can you ensure the guidance provided in or with the diary is written to be understandable to the diarist?
- How can you ensure the guidance provided balances your interest in specific issues with encouragement to diarists to express themselves?
- How can you check that the guidance is comprehensible to the target population?
- Can you provide examples for the diarists of the ways in which diarists have used their diaries?

Contact with diarists

- What are the opportunities to develop a relationship with the diarist, for example briefing meetings, meetings to deliver or collect diaries, debriefing interviews?
- Can you develop a partnership with the diarist based on mutual respect which facilitates mutual understanding of the purposes of the research and the practicalities of keeping the diary?

Checking the nature of the entries

- Is it possible to check a sample entry at an early stage?
- What sort of feedback will be provided?

Summary and comment

The format of diaries and associated guidance for keeping diaries reflect the aims and objectives of the researchers. Researchers engaged in experimental and survey research are concerned with accurate recording of relevant data. The diarist is a surrogate for the researcher and is recording for, on behalf of and to the standards set by the researcher. Thus within this approach to diary research there is a strong emphasis on structuring the diary as a data collecting tool, providing detailed instructions on the ways in which the diary is to be used and checking the accuracy of the data collected.

In contrast the naturalistic researcher is concerned to minimise the impact and intrusiveness of their research into natural social settings. Researchers using unsolicited diaries can achieve this ideal. They have no influence over the ways in which diarists maintained their diary but must decide how far the available diaries meet the needs of their research. Researchers soliciting diaries have to establish a balance. On the one hand they wish to guide the diarist towards the issues or topics that they are interested in, and on the other hand they want to create a user-friendly process that allows diarists to express themself. This can be achieved in a number of ways: the diary itself can be a simple everyday document, such as an exercise book sold in a stationery shop; the guidance can be simple and non-prescriptive; and the researcher can build up a relationship with the diarists. The diary-interview method provides opportunities for building up such a relationship and linking the diary to an in-depth interview.

KEY POINTS

Diaries in experimental and survey research

- *Aim*   To capture accurate unbiased data.
- *The diary*   Formal with maximum use of closed structured data entry.
- *Instructions*   Detailed but comprehensible to the target population.
- *Relationship with diarist*   Surrogate for the researcher.

Unsolicited diaries

- *Aim*   To identify diaries which will provide information that fits the purposes of the research.
- *The diaries*   As written by the diarist and in the form that survives.
- *Instructions*   Not applicable.
- *Relationship with diarist*   The researcher is a user of the document created by the diarist.

Diaries in naturalistic research

- *Aim*   To minimise the distortions which the research process creates in the natural social setting.
- *The diary*   Minimal structure to enable diarists to express themselves.
- *Instructions*   Simple user-friendly informal guidelines.
- *Relationship with diarist*   One of mutual respect in which diarists are treated as equal partners in the research process.

EXERCISE

In the opening context section of this exercise, I outline three potential studies which will use diaries to access appropriate data and information. If you wish to complete the exercise in full then take each study in turn and address the questions set out in the second section. When you have completed all three exercises then turn to the issues set out in the third section. If you are intending to use diaries in a research project then you may wish to substitute your own project for one of the suggested studies.

Three studies

Study I: experimental

A charitable trust has provided funds for a study of teenage pregnancy. The trust wishes to evaluate the impact on sexual activities of two interventions designed to reduce pregnancy: the establishment of an abstinence group among peers, and the provision of sex education plus a free condom service. The agreed research protocol involves recruiting 30 young women (17 years old) and 30 young men (17 years old) and randomly allocating them to one of three groups: the abstinence group, the sex education group and a control group. The diaries are designed to assess the outcome of the experiment in terms of the sexual activities of each group over three two-week periods spread over a six-month period.

Study II: social survey

The public health department of a local health agency wishes to develop its services for young adults. It wants a baseline study of the sexual activities of 300 young women (17 years old) and 300 young men (17 years old) to examine the relationship between peer group relations and other aspects of the social environment, consumption of alcohol, cigarettes and psychoactive drugs, and the use of various measures, including the agency's services, to reduce the risk of pregnancy.

Study III: naturalistic

You have been invited by a women's group to help them develop a diary-based study of women's experience of paid work. The group is particularly interested in the tensions involved in the workplace and between the domestic and paid-work environments. The group has offered to recruit 50 diarists of varied ages and work experience to participate in the study.

(Continued)

(Continued)

Questions for each study

1 *Diary design and structure*

    (a) What are the main issues that you need to consider when designing the research diary?

    (b) Should the diary have a title page? If so, specify what information you need to capture on this page and how you will capture it. Produce a mock title page.

    (c) What time period should each page cover: a week, a day of the week or 24 hours? Justify why you have selected this period.

    (d) How should each diary page be presented? Produce a mock diary page with, as appropriate, a heading and structured data entry sections and/or free text sections. Discuss the advantages and disadvantages of different formats and justify the one which you have used.

2 *Guidance*

    (a) What formats and media can you use to provide guidance for diarists on how to use their diary, e.g. verbal communication, electronic text, printed sheets either included in the diary or free standing, and text printed onto each diary page? Consider the advantages and disadvantages of the different formats.

    (b) Select a strategy for providing guidance for diarists and justify it.

    (c) Produce a mock set of guidance for diarists and justify it.

3 *Contact with diarists*

    (a) Why and how will you maintain contact with your diarists, and what are the purposes of maintaining contact with the diarists?

    (b) Select a strategy for maintaining contact with your diarists and justify it.

    (c) Produce a protocol for maintaining contact.

4 *Feedback and cross-checking*

    (a) How will you gain feedback and will you need to check the accuracy of diary entries?

    (b) Select a strategy for gaining feedback and, if appropriate, checking the accuracy of diary entries, and justify it.

    (c) Produce a protocol for gaining feedback and, if appropriate, checking the accuracy of diary entries, and justify it.

(Continued)

5 *Other sources of information*
   (a) Will you rely solely on the diaries or will you use other methods of accessing data, such as records, observation, questionnaires or interviews?
   (b) If you decide to use other sources of data, how will you link the two sources of information?

6 *Ethical issues*
   (a) What ethical issues does the study raise?
   (b) How will you obtain ethical approval for the study?

Issues to consider if you have completed the exercise for all three studies

7 *Similarities*   What are the similarities between the diaries you have designed for each study, and why are the diaries similar in these respects?

8 *Differences*   What are the differences between the diaries you have designed for each study, and why do the diaries differ in these respects?

5

Analysing Diaries: Numbers, Content and Structure

I do not agree with you that diaries afford the most trustworthy evidence. In them there is always, I feel, an interlocutor – namely, myself, the worst of all interlocutors.

(William Ewart Gladstone, 1896)

Key aims
- To consider the different approaches which can be used to analyse diaries.

Key objectives
- To examine the ways in which researchers can use statistical techniques to analyse the data created by structured diaries.
- To examine the ways in which researchers can analyse the content of diary texts.
- To examine the ways in which researchers can analyse the structure of diary texts.

Alternative approaches to analysing diaries

Structured diaries and the production of numbers

How researchers approach the task of analysis depends on the purpose of their research and their perception of the nature of the entries in the diaries. Researchers engaged in research using experimental or survey methods are usually interested in deduction or theory testing. They will see the data recorded in diaries as representing specific forms of social reality and are interested in identifying and making sense of the patterns within the data. These patterns can most easily be identified when the data are expressed as numbers and therefore the diaries used in experimental and survey research should be structured to facilitate coding, the conversion of the information they contain into numbers (Moser and Kalton, 1971, p. 414). The data within each case are organised into categories or variables, and the data relevant to each variable for each case are coded as a number. This creates a dataset which can be analysed using statistical techniques. The aim of the analysis is to identify relationships between variables and demonstrate that they are unlikely to be a product of chance.

Both experimental and survey research explore the relationship between variables. Experimental research aims to test hypotheses and focuses on the relationship between a limited group of variables: those which represent the intervention, and those which measure the outcome or impact of the intervention. For example, in the data from an experiment which seeks to evaluate the impact of a new treatment for asthma sufferers, one variable will indicate whether the subject was in the control or experimental group while the others will measure outcomes in terms of impact on the patient. In one study outcome was monitored using 32 variables assessing activity limitations, symptoms, emotional function and exposure to environmental stimuli (Fitzpatrick et al., 2001, pp. 182–3). Given the focus of experimental research on a restricted and predetermined range of variables, it is often possible to make strong inferences about their relationship and therefore cause and effect. In contrast, surveys are often more open and extensive; they are not usually oriented towards testing a single hypothesis, but rather seek to identify characteristics of populations. Moser and Kalton have described the two main objectives of surveys in the following way:

(a) The main purpose is generally to *estimate* certain population parameters – the average age of students in college, the proportion of workers in a factory working overtime, and so on …

(b) A second possible purpose may be to *test a statistical hypothesis* about a population – e.g. the hypothesis that at least 80 per cent of households in a town have TV sets. (italics in the original: 1971, p. 62)

Survey researchers are usually interested in a range of variables and may be open to the possibility of new variables emerging as they analyse their data. Given the wide range of variables it is often difficult in survey research to make strong inferences about their relationship and therefore cause and effect (Bolger et al., 2003, p. 587).

Identifying themes: content analysis and grounded theory

Researchers using naturalistic approaches to diaries are interested in qualitative data and tend to use diaries that have an open structure and when complete take the form of written text. In the case of audio and video diaries the researcher has to create this text by transcribing the relevant recordings. The written text created by these diaries does not have the inbuilt structure of diaries used in experimental or survey research. Thus the researcher needs to decide how to manage this text. The text can be treated as providing information on aspects of social reality which are external to the text. The other approach is to treat the text as an end in itself, as a form of social reality that is the product of and provides information on the social processes which underpin its creation and form.

The first approach to text involves some form of content analysis (Brewer, 2003b, p. 43). While the term 'content analysis' can be used to refer to all forms of textual analysis, I use it in a more restricted sense, that of identifying the information contained within the texts which can be used to identify a reality external to the text, whether these be descriptions of a specific event, activity or relation or the diarist's feelings and responses. Content analysis involves taking a number of written texts such as diaries, breaking them into their constituent parts and reassembling these parts into a new scientific text. The starting point for the analysis is the identification of constituent units of the text. If the researcher has a clear idea of what he or she is looking for and expects to find, then they can examine the text to identify relevant characteristics. Franzoni describes this process in the following way:

> In content analysis each characteristic of a text of interest to an investigator is formalized as a 'coding category' – the set of all coding categories known as a 'coding scheme'. The scheme is then systematically applied to a text to extract uniform and standardized information … a coding scheme works like a survey questionnaire administered to a sample of texts rather than to a sample of human respondents. Coder and interviewer play similar roles. In neither case are these figures simple transcribing devices. But in content analysis, the coder plays a greater role in the production of 'data' through interpretation of texts. (2004, p. 4)

While content analysis can create data which can be summarised numerically, it is important to recognise that if the research is designed to create hypotheses and not test them then such numbers will usually indicate general trends within the data rather than the values of specific variables. For example numbers can be used to indicate whether an issue identified in a specific diary is unique to that diary or can be identified in other diaries in the study and if so what proportion of the diaries in the study.

If the researcher does not start with a clear idea of the specific characteristics he or she is interested in then the categories and overall scheme will develop as the researcher investigates and compares texts. Such an approach has been formalised as part of grounded theory, where researchers develop their coding categories through a process of constant comparison (Charmaz, 2003, pp. 257–60):

How do we do grounded theory? Analysis begins early. We grounded theorists code our emerging data as we collect them. Through coding, we start to define and categorize our data. In grounded theory coding, we create codes as we study our data. We do not, or should not, paste catchy concepts on our data. We should interact with our data and pose questions to them while coding them. Coding helps us to gain a new perspective on our material and to focus further data collection, and may lead us in unforeseen directions. Unlike quantitative research that requires data to fit into *preconceived* standardized codes, the researcher's interpretations of data shape his or her emergent codes in grounded theory. (2003, p. 258)

Structural analysis of text: conversational and narrative analysis

Researchers who use content analysis to identify the themes and categories contained within the text have some common ground with researchers using statistical techniques to analyse the numbers generated by structured questions contained within some diaries. Both groups of researchers see the material recorded in the diary as the record of some aspect of social reality that is external to the text they are analysing, and the text describes and can be used to build up a picture of this external reality whatever its precise form, e.g. events, actions, perceptions, emotions. Thus the researcher is concerned about the relationship between the reality as recorded in the text and the reality external to the text. In particular the researcher is concerned to identify the biases and distortions created by the diary keeping process. Researchers using experimental or survey work can introduce 'quality checks', for example electronic recording systems, while researchers using diaries in other forms of research can cross-check or triangulate the information recorded in the diaries with other sources of data (Stake, 2003).

If diaries are treated as records of a competent and disinterested observer then any distortion or bias is a cause for concern. For example, Clarkson noted that documents such as diaries need to be treated with caution:

[They] are tricky; they tell us what the author wants us to know, which is not necessarily what the researcher is really interested in. They offer a version of events from the perspective of the narrator. This is the case even of documents generated officially, but the opportunities for putting a gloss on reality are all the greater in diaries, letters and memoirs. (2003, p. 82)

Similarly Bohman commented on the limitations of documents written by Swedish working men:

He found the diaries, small printed pocket-books crammed with tiny writing, still traditional journals of events, mainly about the weather and work: none took the form of the private reflective diary. (cited in Thompson, 1988, p. 244)

Researchers who are interested in accessing such texts to examine how Swedish working men perceived and responded to their everyday life are

---

(Extract from a conversation between an HIV counsellor (*C*) and a patient (*P*)

```
1  C  Can I just briefly ask why: you thought about having
2     an HIV test done:
3  P  .hh We:ll I mean it's something that you have these
4     I mean that you have to think about these da:ys, and
5     I just uh: m felt (0.8) you- you have had sex with
6     several people and you just don't want to go on (.)
7     not knowing.
```

FIGURE 5.1 *Conversational analysis: a question and answer adjacency pair (Silverman, 1994, p. 72)*

bound to be disappointed. However there is another way of viewing such texts which is as products of specific social processes. The focus then shifts from what the texts tell the researcher about a reality external to and separate from the text to the internal structure of the text. This approach draws on work in linguistics and literary studies exploring the ways in which individuals use and structure text to communicate and present themselves and informs conversational and narrative analysis.

Conversational analysis developed out of the 'ethnomethodological principles of locating and describing the methods and techniques that people use to produce and interpret social interaction' (Acton, 2003, p. 49). As the term implies, the technique is primarily concerned with naturally occurring talk and in identifying and analysing the features of such talk, especially the social conventions which underpin and shape social interaction (see Bryman, 2001, pp. 354–60). Diaries lack the multiplicity of voices that are present in conversation and written diaries do not need transcribing. However it is possible to treat diaries either as records of interactions or as a form of interaction. For example Alan Bennett, the British playwright and diarist, described his diaries 'like conversations, in fact, even if conversations with oneself' (1998, p. 133). If diaries are treated as texts which are the product of a naturally occurring method of communication, it is likely that they will have conventions similar to those which underpin other naturally occurring forms of communication and therefore diaries should be amenable to some aspects of conversational analysis.

Conversational analysis is a sophisticated way of presenting and analysing naturally occurring communication. For example Silverman provides an example of an adjacency pair – two linked phases in talk such as question and answer (see Figure 5.1).

Narrative analysis has been applied to written texts, particularly ones which are 'first-person accounts by respondents of their experiences' (Riessman, 1993, p. 1).

While the approach has been developed in the context of in-depth interviews, there appears to be no reason why it should not be applied to diaries.

Researchers using narrative analysis are interested in identifying the structure which underpins specific narratives and the ways in which these structures enable the narrator to make sense of and present their lives, especially where 'there has been a breach between ideal and real, self and society' (1993, p. 3). Riessman described the approach in the following way:

> The purpose is to see how respondents … impose order on the flow of experience to make sense of events and actions in their lives. The methodological approach examines the informant's story and analyzes how it is put together, the linguistic and cultural resources it draws on, and how it persuades a listener of authenticity. (1993, p. 2)

Riessman suggested that there was no fixed formula for narrative analysis, rather a set of questions that were used to explore the text. These included the ways in which the text was created; if it was based on talk, how it was transcribed; what aspects of the narrative contained in the text form the basis for its interpretation; and how the text was used, who determined its meaning and whether alternative interpretations were possible (1993, p. 25).

Comment

Researchers who use diaries for experimental and survey research tend to see them as a way of collecting information. They structure the diaries to ensure that the diarist records relevant information accurately and unambiguously so that the information can be easily converted into numbers. They can use statistical analysis to identify relationships between variables and demonstrate that such relationships are unlikely to be the product of chance. Researchers using unsolicited diaries or diaries with open structures have to manage and analyse written text. The researcher can treat the text as a source of information on some aspect of social reality which is recorded in the text. They will want to analyse the content of each diary by identifying common themes in each text and isolating and comparing the information in each text. If the researcher starts with a hypothesis this will provide a framework for the identification of categories that form the basis of a coding frame. This frame can be used to convert the content of the text into numbers. However if the researcher does not start with a specific hypothesis then the categories used can be developed through a process of constant comparison of text: each new text is considered in terms of the themes identified in previous texts, and as new themes are identified the previous texts are reconsidered. An alternative approach is to examine the form and structure of each text. The text is treated not as a potentially distorted reflection of a reality external to the text, 'the world out there' (Riessman, 1993, pp. 3–4), but as a social phenomenon in its own right. The focus is on how this phenomenon is created, the underpinning process. In conversational analysis the relationship is more on social conventions embedded in the text. In narrative analysis the focus is on the way in which the text is structured and used.

Box 5.1 Alternative strategies for analysing diaries

Numerical analysis

- Identification of variables
- Coding of specific data related to variables to create numbers
- Statistical analysis of variables
- Use of analysis to test or generate hypotheses

Content analysis

- Creation where necessary of texts through transcription
- Identification of categories through reading of texts
- Comparison of different texts to identify material relevant to categories
- Synthesis of categories into a new scientific text

Structural analysis

- Creation, where necessary, of texts through transcription
- Consideration of context in which text was created
- Holistic approach in which each text is treated as an entity
- Identification of structure and method of narration of each text
- Identification of the rules used to construct the text

Identifying numerical patterns: statistical analysis in experimental and survey research

Coding: converting data into numbers

Researchers using diaries for experimental and survey research need, at a very early stage, to start thinking about how they are going to analyse the data, convert them into numbers through a coding system and explore relationships between these numbers using statistical packages. These issues affect the selection of the sample and the design and structure of the diary:

> You should be fully aware of what techniques you will apply at a fairly early stage – for example when you are designing [data collection tools]. The two main reasons for this are as follows.
>
> - You cannot apply just any technique to any variable …
> - The size and nature of your sample are likely to impose limitations on the kinds of technique you can use. (Bryman, 2001, pp. 214–15)

Researchers need to ensure that their diaries are structured in such a way that the data can be easily coded. One way of doing this is to organise the diary as a series of mini-questionnaires which need to be completed at set or agreed times (see for example Bolger et al., 2003). With this approach the researcher needs to decide how to measure each aspect of social reality they are interested in, i.e. what question to ask, and the coding frame, how numbers are to be assigned to answers.

Some phenomena are more complex and difficult and coding the answer is more challenging. For example Bolger et al. (2003), in their review of diaries in psychological research, proposed a diary study to examine the hypothesis that mother's intimacy with their spouse declined following the birth of their first child. Researchers would need to define how intimacy would be measured. Bolger et al. provide an initial definition: 'Intimacy is defined as an individual's feeling of being understood, validated, and cared for by another individual' (2003, p. 586). Such a definition would then need to be turned into specific questions with coding frames for each answer.

Coxon (1996) in his account of Project SIGMA provided a detailed desciption of the ways the research team coded entries in the sexual diaries. The basic structure of the diary was event based, i.e. diarists were invited to make an entry each time a sexual act took place. In the first phase of the Project SIGMA diary study, the team did not specify in detail how diarists should describe each session and diarists used their own term for aspects of the sexual act. For example, diarists used more than five terms to refer to 'penis' and more than three for 'anal intercourse'. In subsequent diaries the team specified the terms which they wanted diarists to use in their descriptions of the sexual act (see Chapter 4).

The Project SIGMA team developed a very clear schema for analysing the components of sexual behaviour. The team defined the basic unit of sexual behaviour as a 'sexual session'. Coxon used a linguistic analogy to specify such units:

> The sexual session may be considered as the 'sentence' of sexual activity – self-sufficient and intrinsically well-formed. (1996, p. 21)

Each sexual session was specified in terms of four components, which provided the context for the core component, the sexual act (1996). The four contextualising components were the setting of the act, its antecedents, its accompaniments and the partner specification. Each of these components involved specifications or descriptions which could be used to code the data. These specifications were clearly outlined in the instructions for writing diaries (1996, p. 177).

This framework provided an effective way of organising a powerful tool for analysing the information recorded in the diaries. Not only could the data from each session be broken into specific variables and the nature of the relationship between variables be identified, but the actual structure of each sexual act could be represented in a symbolic form, facilitating a comparison of sexual acts (1996, pp. 183–4).

Making sense of the numbers: statistical analysis

Once the researchers have coded the information that they identify in each diary, they then have to extract and store these numbers, statistically analyse them and decide how they will treat and code missing data. This usually means entering data into a statistical software package on a computer system such as SPSS or Minitab (for a guide on how to use SPSS for Windows see Bryman, 2001, pp. 239–59). It is important to ensure that data are entered accurately. Data derived from traditional paper and pen diaries have to be manually coded and entered. This is both time consuming and a potential source of error. Usually a sample of the data is entered twice to check the accuracy of the data entry (Bolger et al., 2003, p. 594). One way of reducing cost and increasing accuracy is to use electronic diaries which automatically code entries and which often have facilities for preventing ineligible answers and ensuring all questions are answered by presenting them in sequence each time the diary is used (2003, p. 594).

Once the data are entered the researcher needs to decide how to identify and explore the relationship between variables. The researcher can start by identifying the independent variables in the data, i.e. those which are not dependent on other variables (Cooper, 2003, p. 10) and then exploring the relationship between these independent variables:

> In quantitative data analysis a statistical interaction can be defined as an expression of the linkage or association between two or more independent/causal variables. This linkage is beyond what would be expected by chance. (Miller, 2003b, p. 306)

The type of techniques the researcher chooses to use to explore these relationships depends on the nature of the numbers in each variable, for example in an interval/ratio variable 'the distances between categories are identical across the range of categories' (Bryman, 2001, p. 219). Thus the difference between 1 and 2 and between 6 and 7 in a variable based on a measure of time such as minutes is the same. In contrast, for nominal variables the allocation of numbers is essentially arbitrary and merely signifies difference. For example Bryman gives an example of a coding system for a questionnaire on the use of a gym in which responses to the question on the 'main reason for going to the gym' were numerically coded, with 'relaxation' coded as 1 and 'maintain or improve fitness' as 2 and so on (2001, p. 218). The researcher's choice of statistical techniques will also be influenced by the purposes of the research and the types of audience for the findings of the study. The researcher can use relatively simple univariate analysis in which one variable is analysed at a time; bivariate analysis in which two variables are compared; or multivariate analysis in which the relationships between more than two variables are compared. In all these techniques the findings can be presented both visually as graphs or diagrams, and numerically as tables. Less complex statistics tend to be easier to present visually. For example, the products of univariate analyses can be presented as bar charts, pie charts and histograms. Bivariate analyses can be presented as scatter diagrams, while it may be more difficult to present the results of multi-variate analyses visually.

Coxon in his analysis of the Project SIGMA diaries used a variety of statistical techniques. In his analysis of sexual sessions he started with the simple descrip-tion of the length of each sexual session in terms of number of acts per session. He observed that:

> The average (mean) is quite low (1.75 for most data-sets), but there is a very long tail: some sessions are quite long, and a few very long. (1996, p. 109)

He then moved onto more complex analysis to explore the structure of acts, i.e. the relationship between different sex acts. He used multidimensional scaling (Coxon, 1982) to produce a table (1996, Table 6.4) of the co-occurrence of sex acts and a map in which each act was positioned to indicate its association with other acts, i.e. the closer the position the more frequent the covariance. Using this analysis, Coxon was able to explore the relationship between sex acts, show-ing that some acts such as oral sex tended to be reciprocal whereas others such as penetrative sex tended to be asymmetric or 'gendered' (1996, p. 112).

Diary data do have one obvious distinctive feature. Most data used in exper-imental and survey research are synchronic, i.e. a snapshot at a particular moment in time. Diary data are longitudinal or diachronic; they represent a sequence of recordings. Thus these data can be used to explore both group and individual variations over time. Parkin and his colleagues (2004) used exploratory analy-sis to examine the ways in which the symptoms of individuals with relapsing-remitting multiple sclerosis varied over time. The cross-sectional time-series data enabled them to analyse the stability and variability of their main measur-ing instrument, the Euroqol Visual Analogue Scale (EQ VAS: 2004, p. 351). They explored the variation in the scores over time and found that health status scores were stable over time and that 'greater variations in scores were observed between individuals rather than within individuals' (Parkin et al., 2004, p. 351).

Comment

Researchers using diaries for experimental and survey research need to start thinking about and planning data analysis as early as possible so that they build the coding system into the structure of the diary. This ensures that the data contained in each diary can be converted into numbers and that these numbers can be entered into appropriate computer-based statistical packages which can then be used to manipulate these data. Since researchers need to understand

and manage both the practical and the conceptual problems associated with statistical analysis, they should access advice and guidance as early as possible in their study to ensure that they are aware of the coding issues at an early stage of their research.

Box 5.2 Statistical analysis of diary data

Advice

- If you are not an expert in statistics, take advice as early as possible from someone who is

Coding frame

- Identify main variables and ways of measuring them as early as possible
- Build measurement and coding into the structure of the diary
- Ensure data can be transferred easily from diary into the data storage and analysis system, if possible via an electronic system

Coding data

- Convert any outstanding written text into numbers
- Transfer all data into the storage and analysis system
- Check accuracy of transfer by re-entering a sample of data

Statistical analysis

- Consider how and why you want to analyse the data, especially what relationships are likely to be important
- Start with simplest forms of analysis and consider the results before proceeding to more complex forms
- Consider what sorts of statistical analyses are appropriate for the different variables
- Consider how you can present the findings in ways that are easy to understand

---

Analysing the content of diaries

Researchers using diaries for experimental and survey research can build the coding system into the structure of the diary so that such diaries take the form of a series of mini-questionnaires. There may be space for free text but such text can also be converted into numbers. Researchers using unsolicited diaries or soliciting diaries for naturalistic research either cannot rigidly structure the diaries or prefer to avoid doing so. The first task is to convert and enter this text into a form that can be managed, which is relatively straightforward for written diaries but may be more complex for audio or audiovisual diaries, and the second stage is to identify themes and relationship between themes.

Converting diaries into text

Converting written diaries into text is usually a relatively straightforward process of typing the text using a word processing package. The researcher needs to decide which features of the original layout should be included. For example, should gaps in the text, emphases or underlining be transcribed, and if so how? Generally these conventions are relatively easy to establish and use systematically. However matters become more complex when audio or audiovisual diaries are transcribed. Such diaries include not only words but also pauses and inflections, and in audiovisual diaries there may also be accompanying expressions or gestures. Again the researcher needs to decide what is to be transcribed and what conventions need to be used. Generally researchers who are interested in the natural context and diary conventions will seek to record as much 'background' information as possible. Within conversational analysis, researchers have developed a series of conventions to capture the content and structure of natural talk. These conventions are designed to show how the interaction works:

> Pauses, silences, overlaps, laughter, applause, tone and volume are just some features that are transcribed in an attempt to capture not only the content of talk, but also the way in which it is produced. The key features of a recording are rarely apparent on the first hearing and the analytic process therefore involves repeated listening to the original tape recording in order to become familiar with the complexities of the interaction. (Acton, 2003, p. 51)

These conventions can inform the transcription of audio and audiovisual diaries. For example Papadopoulos and Scanlon (2002) used audio diaries in an exploratory study designed to document a day in the life of four individuals with visual impairment. Although the published account of the work does not provide detailed information on the transcription, the authors indicated that they 'paid particular attention to the participants' tone and volume of voice, silence gaps, other sounds or voices' (2002, p. 457) when listening to the tapes and transcribing.

Identifying themes in text

When the contents of the diary have been transcribed, the process of identifying themes can begin. This process involves scrutinising the text, reading and rereading it, to identify and confirm themes and to organise and synthesise all the evidence relevant to each theme. Prior to the development of computer-based software, organising text involved the physical manipulation of text, cutting up sections of text and pasting them on cards that could be grouped together into themes and then families of themes. There is now a variety of software packages that electronically 'cut-and-paste' text such as QSR NVivo or ATLAS.ti (see Bryman, 2001, p. 407).

The precise starting point depends on the nature of the project. Researchers who start with clearly defined hypotheses which they have derived from previous studies or theoretical analyses often have a clear set of issues which they want to test against data they have collected (Brewer, 2003c, p. 154). They can search relevant texts looking for evidence which confirms or disproves their hypothesis. For example Pollock (1983) in her diary study of parent–child relationships initially identified and read a range of documents to identify those which included accounts of child–adult relations. She then focused on these accounts to examine how they conceptualised childhood and if so what form it took, whether they contained information on the discipline and control of children, and whether this involved violence. The use of such evidence enabled Pollock to conclude that:

> The information provided by the sources reveals that parents, through the centuries studied, have tried to control, or at least regulate, their children's behaviour ... The methods used to discipline a child varied according to the parent and child rather than the time period, with the possible exception of the early 19th century – in every century strict and indulgent parents appeared ... Parents did wish, in theory, to have a great deal of authority over their children, but in practice they did not achieve that aim. (1983, p. 199)

An alternative approach is based on developing generalisations and theories from the data by being ' "true to the data themselves", allowing the data "to speak for themselves" ' (Brewer, 2003c, p. 154). This approach underpins grounded theory which, while it does acknowledge the possibility of deduction using 'theoretical categories', is primarily oriented towards induction, developing categories out of a systematic inspection of the text (Charmaz, 2003, pp. 258–9; Strauss and Corbin, 1990).

Griffith and Jordan (1998) used this approach in their exploratory diary-interview study of patients' experiences during recovery from lower limb fracture. The study was based on a convenience sample of nine patients who were recovering from emergency surgery following a lower limb trauma. The researchers used a grounded theory approach, independently reading the texts and identifying categories. From their analysis they identified three major themes which they found were concordant with a theoretical model evident in the literature:

> The diaries were initially read through, to form provisional headings and tentative categories, which were confirmed or rejected at the final interview. Further categories were induced by analysing the data on the 'Ethnograph' software package, case by case ... As each case was analysed, themes emerged from these categories. Coding was undertaken sequentially by the authors, with the final categories reflecting joint decisions. Three dominant themes emerged, stress and uncertainty, seeking control and returning to normal; these were concordant with Lazarus's model of stress and coping. (1998, p. 1278)

Griffith and Jordan provided a summary of their main themes and subthemes (see Figure 5.2).

Theme 1: dealing with uncertainty – the stressors	Theme 2: seeking control – appraising and coping	Theme 3: returning to 'normality' – adaptation
Shock and pain experienced	Seeking familiarity	Balance between rest and activity
An alien environment	Seeking control	Returning to normality
Seeking suitable medication		
Fear of falling		
Worrying about recovering		
Mastering use of crutches		

FIGURE 5.2 *Themes and subthemes identified by Griffith and Jordan in their diary study (adapted from Griffith and Jordan, 1998, p. 1278)*

Using software packages

While it now virtually inconceivable that numerical data could be analysed without using a statistical software package, computer-assisted qualitative data analysis is a more recent development. For example the prototype of ATLAS was developed as part of an interdisciplinary project between 1989 and 1992 and is a multimedia package. A commercial version was launched in 1993 and a DOS version for Windows in 1997 (Muhr, 1997, p. 5). There is now a number of software packages that can be used to help in the analysis of qualitative data. For example Bryman (2001, p. 407) in his review of computer-assisted analysis identifies five main packages: The Ethnograph, QSR N6 (NUD*IST), QSR NVivo, winMAX and ATLAS.ti. (At the time of writing, information on these packages and access to demonstration models could be found through the SCOLARI website, http://www.scolari.co.uk). As Bryman (2001) provides a useful introduction to using NVivo I will concentrate on ATLAS.ti.

While such packages facilitate the process of managing qualitative data and help with analysis, they require a substantial investment of time to master and use effectively and they do not remove the need for researchers to use their judgement when identifying themes:

> The fundamental design objective we applied when creating ATLAS/ti was a tool which effectively supports the human interpreter, particularly in handling relatively large amounts of research material, notes, and associated theories. (Muhr, 1997, p. 4)

The first step in using ATLAS.ti is to enter the text or other qualitative data into the software system. Each diary should be entered and should form a separate primary document. Once text has been entered, the researcher can begin to analyse it. The researcher should read and code each document. The codes are words or short pieces of text added to the margin of a unit to identify and mark longer sections of text. The code can be used as a keyword or index to identify and retrieve all text marked with this code from all specified units, an electronic cut-and-paste. Codes can be grouped into clusters or families or into more complex hierarchical structures or networks which contain nodes and links.

> ATLAS/ti uses networks to help explore conceptual structures and make them transparent. The networks add a heuristic 'right brain' approach to qualitative research. (1997, p. 129)

We used ATLAS.ti to analyse the data from a diary-interview study of the ways in which younger people responded to and managed the consequence of a stroke (Alaszewski and Alaszewski, 2005). Following an initial interview, stroke survivors and carers were invited to keep a diary for one week per month for three six-month periods. After we had transcribed an initial batch of five diaries, the first step in our analysis was to identify themes and issues within these diaries. Since this was essentially an exploratory phase we started with printed copies of a single diary. Two members of the research team independently read transcripts of the diary, marking units of the text with coloured highlighter pen and making notes and comments in the margin. From this initial reading both readers prepared a list of the main themes and the issues which they classified under each theme. They then compared their lists and agreed a new list of themes (see Figure 5.3). This was a relatively straightforward task involving in some cases a change in the title of themes and in other cases the addition of themes which one reader had identified and the other had not. For example, reader 1 had identified fatigue as a major theme. Reader 2 had also identified fatigue, but saw it as a subcategory within the overall theme of 'aftermath of stroke'. While both readers had identified fatigue as a category, they differed in how they classified it. Following discussion they decided to identify it as a subtheme within the overall theme of aftermath of stroke, as it was clearly important and it had both physical and psychological dimensions and so could not be classified in the other two subthemes (see Figure 5.3).

The next stage of the process was to enter the diary into the software package and to begin to use the agreed themes and categories in marking up the text. Once each diary had been entered into ATLAS.ti and coded, we could begin to compare the diaries. For example after we had entered and coded four diaries we identified a theme related to cars and driving. Using ATLAS.ti it was relatively simple to identify all the references to cars and driving. When these were brought together a clear pattern was evident. Diarists who made driving-related entries experienced the loss of ability to drive as a major disability reducing their autonomy and independence, and reacquiring this facility was a major objective whose accomplishment created considerable satisfaction and was treated as sign of recovery and progress back to normality (see Figure 5.4).

Reader 1	Reader 2	Agreed
1 Fatigue: • saving up energy • need rest • associated with symptoms	1 Aftermath of stroke: • physical feelings, fatigue, pain, numbness • psychological, anxiety, moods, memory loss	1 Aftermath of stroke: • physical symptoms, pain in leg, headaches • psychological symptoms, anxiety, moods, anger • fatigue
2 Domestic/family: • activity round house, pressure of not being able to help • active, contributing in house	2 Family and other relationships: • loss of role, guilt about children, self-justification • support, husband take on lot of role, help children and friends	2 Family and social support: • loss of role, guilt about children, self-justification • support, husband take on lot of role, help children and friends • social activity, important, preserving energy for, positive feelings about
3 Contact professionals: • physio *re* tiredness • neurologist prescribes drugs • loss of PT who she gets on with	3 Professional support: • interventions, medication, reassurance, exercises • talking	3 Professional advice/support: • professionals, neurologist, PT, OT, nurse • treatments, medication, exercise • advice and counselling, way sought, response to
4 Independence: • want to get back to driving • relieve husband of pressure • loss of job	4 Getting back to normal: • cooking/ domestic chores • getting the bus, driving • going shopping	4 Strategies for getting back to normal: • domestic sphere, cooking, chores, normal family relations

(Continued)

(Continued)		
Reader 1	Reader 2	Agreed
		• accessing environment, via friends, bus, driving • paid employment, loss, desire to get back • day-to-day, pushing self, conserving energy, focusing
5 Challenges: • normal family life • driving • overcome fatigue to socialise	5 Management: • pushing self • rationing energy in planning?	5 Evaluating progress: • types of evaluation, symptoms, moods, achievements, failures • positive experiences, less symptoms, more energy, challenges met • negative experiences, anger, disability allowance, loss of occupation
6 Symptoms: • headaches • pain in left foot • balancing family and symptoms		
7 Good day/positive experience: • effort rewarded • less symptoms • more energy		
8 Bad day/negative feelings: • family pressure • anger after bad hair cut • loss of work		

FIGURE 5.3   *Initial reading of text and identification of themes and categories (categories shortened and only three examples given)*

	Mrs J.'s diary
1	I will be glad now to get back to driving as I feel a lot better and feel I can manage it (in small doses, as I still get tired easily).
2	Friday Pete's day off – so I went to the schools with the kids and then to the doctor's surgery as I wanted to ask the doctor about returning to driving! And she said go ahead? I was surprised that she didn't need to do any tests, like eyes, balance etc., although I know myself whether I am fit enough for it or not. I informed the DVLA and insurance and had a little test drive with Pete next to me and it was fine!

	Mrs H.'s (carer) diary
1	She will find out all she can for Mr H. and sort out physio for hand and arm and exercises and therapy for driving.
2	Mary from CART brought round putty for Mr H. to exercise his fingers, gave him tasks to do; all to help him to get back driving but without Mr H. realising it so he doesn't get his hopes up but he goes on about driving quite a bit.
3	Mary and Jane 2 p.m. assess Mr H. for driving.
4	Thursday 8 July Mary and Jane started to look at exercises? To help him towards driving.

	Mrs T.'s diary
1	My best friend came down today and sorted out my finances for me. I have been getting in such a state with money. She helped me out such a lot and I think I may have sold my car which will be a great help for my money problems. I have got to ring this fellow back on Saturday so we have all got our fingers crossed!!
2	We ended up calling in at Tesco's on the way home which was good as I wanted some photos done in one of them booths to send off for my disabled parking ticket.
3	But I have a busy day ahead. My friend is coming down to help me with my bills. Also my son is coming down to take my car over to Sea Bay to sell it to a garage whom I phoned up yesterday. He told me over the phone as long as it is in A1 condition he would be able to give me £500 for it but it depended on what he found when he saw it. Anyway, while my son was on his way over my friend and I were working out my finances. Then the dreaded phone-call from my son came. Man said he will only give me £250, the wheel-arch was badly rusted and some-thing else he found wrong so I said regretfully, grab his hand before he finds something else so that is what he did. I told my friend and told her that £200 of that would put me back on track with the bank so we all agreed.

FIGURE 5.4 *Extract from four diaries using ATLAS.ti (one diary did not have any relevant entries)*

Comment

Researchers who use diaries as a record of phenomena outside the diary tend to treat each diary as a collection of information and therefore scrutinise the text to identify the types of information it contains. This involves reading and rereading the text. While the researcher may seek to treat the texts as providing insight into a new social phenomenon, analysis usually starts with and is influenced by the findings of previous research in the same or related areas. Since analysis requires the exercise of judgement about the types of information or themes that can be identified in the text, it is usual for more than one researcher to be involved in the process so that judgements can be compared and contrasted and inconsistencies identified and examined. Initial categorisation is treated as provisional and subject to refinement and change as the researchers develop their analyses and apply the categories to each new text. As the analysis progresses so each diary or text is divided up into its constituent parts, and these are subsequently brought together and synthesised to construct a new understanding of specific social phenomena.

Box 5.3 Analysing the content of unsolicited diaries or diaries with open structures

Transcribing and entering text

- Decide whether you are going to use a computer-assisted analysis package, select a package and ensure that you have training or appropriate assistance in using the package
- Identify the key features of the text which you wish to preserve in addition to the words, e.g. layout, breaks in text, emphases, and decide on the ways these features will be identified in the transcribed text
- Convert the material in the diary into typed text using the prescribed conventions
- If appropriate, enter the text into the data analysis software package

Developing the coding system

- Read and reread the text, provisionally identifying themes and issues
- Provisionally mark text and place code or comments alongside marked text
- Ensure at least a sample of the text is read and marked by another researcher
- When coding system is agreed, code all text

Synthesising data

- Group all text in relevant codes and consider similarities and differences between text placed in the same code
- Group similar and related codes together, examining the links and relationships between categories
- Identifying overarching themes and issues

Working with the text: identifying the underlying structure

Researchers using a structural approach are concerned with maintaining the integrity of each text. They are interested in identifying the structure which underpins each text, the differences between the structures of similar texts such as diaries, and the reasons why such structure exists. This requires identifying and retaining the essential quality or structure of each text, and in this section I will discuss two approaches to such analysis: conversational analysis and narrative analysis.

Conversational analysis

Researchers who use conversational analysis are interested in the patterns of everyday social interactions and with 'uncovering the underlying structures of talk in interaction and as such with the achievement of order through interaction' (Bryman, 2001, p. 355). Conversational analysis focuses on the conventions which underpin social interaction and can be used to explore the ways in which diaries represent and record social interaction.

Jones and his colleagues (Jones et al., 2000; Jones and Candlin, 2003) used diaries to explore the ways in which men who have sex with other men accounted for their actions. They recruited 18 gay men who kept diaries in which they recorded their sexual activities and their reflections on sex and AIDS. In these diaries they identified 49 'sexual narratives' which they defined as 'accounts of specific sexual encounters with specific partners in specific settings which contained three or more clauses arranged in chronological order' (2003, p. 203). They found that the narratives had a distinctive form; accounts were presented as 'paired actions' 'which helped portray their risk behavior as somehow justified, reasonable, or even inevitable' (2003, p. 203).

Jones and Candlin argued that the structure of these narratives was equivalent to a 'silent conversation' in which each action simultaneously displays evidence on how previous actions should be interpreted and creates opportunities for subsequent actions. The text was:

> a cumulative construction of identity and interactional 'rights' driven by the pair-wise organization of the interaction. Through these sequences of actions, characters are seen as exchanging claims and imputations of discourse identity which serve as the basis for claims and imputations of social identity. (2003, p. 204)

The underlying binary structure of most of the diaries was analysed and displayed as a sequence of exchanges.

Narrative analysis

Narrative analysis also explores the structure of the text but, rather than focusing on the structures of interactions which underpin the text, it addresses the ways in which the narrator structures and uses the narrative, especially the role of the author in telling the story in a convincing way. Thus narrative analysis is interested in the production of the text, the identity and intention of its author, the extent to which the author appears in the text and the devices used in the text.

Geertz (1988) used this approach to explore the ways in which ethnographers constructed and formed their accounts of other cultures they had studied and wanted to represent to members of their own culture. The texts he used included diaries such as Malinowski's (see Chapter 2). Geertz started his analysis by noting that ethnographic texts tended to have a rather different form to that of other scientific texts. Drawing on Foucault's (1979) analysis of the author function in discourse he noted that author function in ethnographic texts tended to be strong, which emphasised their similarity to other texts with a strong author function, especially fiction but also history, biography, philosophy and poetry, and differentiated them from texts in which the author function tended to be weak, especially scientific texts. He argued that the structure of ethnographic text reflects the difficulties of writing ethnography which involves 'the oddity of constructing texts ostensibly scientific out of experiences broadly biographical, which is after all what ethnographers do' (1988, p. 10).

Crossley (2003) used this approach to analyse John Diamond's diary. This diary was originally published as a weekly column in *The Times* and then as part of a posthumous collection of Diamond's writings (2001, see also Diamond, 1999). It told the story of Diamond's illness and death from oral cancer. Crossley treated Diamond's 'diary' as a text in which the author sought to make sense of challenges to his very existence (2003, p. 441). Crossley identified four distinctive devices that structure the text and its story. The first related to the early pre-cancer stage in which Diamond raised the possibility of cancer but distanced himself from the experience:

> Using the past tense, 'I *thought* I *had*' … immediately signals to the reader that Diamond believed something that turned out to be incorrect. (italics in Crossley's text: 2003, p. 441)

The second device used during earlier periods of treatment involved an emphasis on the realities of being diagnosed and treated for oral cancer. Crossley (2003, p. 443) noted the ways in which Diamond used his 'diary' as a way of coping with his illness and engaged in an active process of emplotment, concentrating on the details of the diagnosis and the treatment so that the underlying anxiety and uncertainty was marginalised and held at bay:

> At times, Diamond's fears about his future slip through, but for the most part, he does not allow himself to look beyond the horizon of the specific treatment, and focuses his sights on the hoped for outcome – recovery. (2003, p. 443)

The third device, used during periods of remission, was to avoid writing about the cancer. Following the completion of his initial treatment, Diamond made few references in his diary column to cancer. Crossley notes that, 'It is almost as if he is holding his breath, waiting, in limbo, too scared even to mention it' (2003, p. 444).

The final device involved an articulation of the 'unspoken narrative', the acknowledgement of uncertainty and fear and the associated loss of faith in treatment and a return to health. Towards the end of his diary columns Diamond wrote, 'There are times when I feel I'm covering a long and particularly futile war' (Crossley, 2003, p. 445). Crossley argued that Diamond used such devices to structure and communicate his experience of cancer. The authenticity of his account was created by the progression from initial distancing through alternation between therapeutic emplotment and avoidance to the final unspoken narrative.

Box 5.4 Analysing the structure of diaries

Identify and prepare texts

- Decide on the unit(s) of analysis, i.e. what will constitute a single text for the purposes of the study
- If the text does not already exist as a published or printed document, convert the material in the diary into typed text using the prescribed conventions

Identify the structure

- Decide what approach you wish to take to the text, e.g. conversational or narrative analysis
- Read and reread each text, identifying key features such as voice of author, appeal to reader, presentation of events

Explore how and why the structure is used

- Consider context of document
- Compare similarities and variations in structure

Comment

Structural analysis involves treating each diary as a unique and integrated text and examining the ways in which the author structures the text. This structuring is treated as a social process in its own right which can provide information on the ways in which the author manages and creates an account of his or her activity, the nature of social interactions and exchanges represented in the text and the mechanisms of communication such as establishing the authenticity of the text and the credibility of its author. Conversational analysis focuses on the pattern of social interactions and exchanges in the text and explores the ways in which they are used in the text. Narrative explores the role of the author in 'telling a story', the devices which the author uses to make the narrative understandable and credible, especially when the author and the reader do not share common experiences, for example the ethnographer seeking to communicate about another culture and the cancer sufferer or survivor trying to explain what it feels like to have cancer.

Summary and comment

The analysis of data is often the most exciting and enjoyable part of the research process. In the early stages there is a lot of preparatory work and uncertainty, but as the researcher begins to engage with and analyse the data and begins to identify patterns and the overall shape of the main findings, so all the investment in preparation begins to pay off.

This may explain some of the attractions of structural analysis and content analysis using grounded theory. The researcher does not have to wait until all the data have been collected but can get started with the analysis as soon as one diary or text has been collected, and then the analysis develops as other texts are identified, indeed the analysis of texts can influence the subsequent selection of texts. By contrast, researchers using quantitative data have to wait until all the data are collected and have been entered into the statistical package and cleaned before they can begin to explore the patterns in their data sets. Bryman (2001, p. 63) identifies 11 steps in quantitative research, with analysis as the ninth.

Key points

Data from structured diaries

- *Type of data*   Numbers.
- *Units of analysis*   Variables which as far as possible are built into the structure of the diaries.
- *Supports for analysis*   Statistical packages such as SPSS.
- *Presentation of findings*   Tables of numbers, in visual forms such as graphs, and results of statistical tests.

Analysis of the content of diaries

- *Type of data*   Primarily text.
- *Units of analysis*   Coding categories which can be grouped into themes.
- *Supports for analysis*   Traditional cut-and-paste or computer-assisted qualitative data analysis packages such as ATLAS.ti.
- *Presentation of findings* Usually as a scientific narrative supported by extracts from texts illustrating categories and themes and some simple numerical data.

Structural analysis of diaries

- *Type of data*   Text.
- *Units of analysis*   Each individual text.
- *Supports for analysis*   Concepts from literary studies on the construction of text.
- *Presentation of findings* An account of the structure of the text with illustrations from specific texts.

EXERCISE

Within the context of this book, it is difficult to provide sufficient data to make an analysis exercise interesting and meaningful. Therefore the following exercises are designed to highlight some of the issues you will need to think about if you intend to use diaries.

Exercise 1: quantitative data analysis

The study

A charitable trust has provided funds for a study of safe sex. The trust wishes to monitor the pattern of sexual activity among young adults to assess whether condom use is related to stated preferences and the extent to which they feel they have control over sexual activity.
The study involves a questionnaire (questions A and B) and a simple sexual diary with instructions.

A   How important is it for you to have safe sex (sex using a condom)?
        Very important _____
        Fairly important _____

(Continued)

(Continued)

       Not very important _____
       Not at all important _____

B Do you consider you have a stable relationship (steady boyfriend or
    girlfriend)?
      Yes _____
      No _____

Instructions

For each day please record each occasion on which you had physical
contact with a member of the opposite sex. For each occasion please
record the partner, particularly his or her age (if you do not know,
please estimate), the status of your partner (for example if he is your
boyfriend or girlfriend, or someone you have known for some time or
you have just met), what happened (e.g. petting, foreplay, vaginal
penetration, anal penetration), condoms (was one used, did you
discuss use, how was the decision made to use or not use).

Issues to consider

While some of the issues will be clarified if and when you collect the
data, it is possible to begin to think about the analysis at this stage by
considering the following issues:

1 What are the main variables that you can identify?
2 Can you outline a coding frame for each variable?
3 Can you differentiate between the variables in terms of the
    numbers, for example can you identify interval/ratio, ordinal,
    nominal and dichotomous variables?
4 What sort of analysis will you want to undertake – univariate,
    bivariate or multivariate – and why?
5 Will it be important that the results are statistically significant, and
    if so why?

Exercises 2 and 3: content analysis and structural analysis

The study

A national charity has provided funding for a longitudinal study of the
ways in which younger stroke survivors reconstruct their lives following
a stroke. The study involves three interview/diary/reinterview cycles
over a period of 18 months starting within 12 weeks of the stroke. The

participants are invited to keep a diary for one week per month over the 18-month period. The following extracts have been taken from four first-cycle diaries, i.e. from the first six-month cycle. Preceding each extract is background information on the diarist. I have selected extracts which focus on a similar theme.

In the first exercise you are invited to analyse the content of each extract, and in the second the structure.

Extract 1

Mr N. is a 58-year-old man who had a stroke about four months before this entry. He has a right hemiparesis and some expressive dysphasia. He lives with his wife and was active and in employment prior to the stroke. He is unable to write and dictates the diary to his wife.

Thursday 1 April
I am now able to wash, dress and fasten my watch (after much practice). The CART team come most days. I think it helps, but it's not really physio and the progress is too slow. My right hand is pretty useless, but mobility is just OK. It's mostly self-help. I felt pretty low sometimes over the last few weeks, especially when I had to rely on a neighbour and friend to creosote the fence.

My wife tries to get me out most days and we had a ride out and pub lunch last week.

Extract 2

Mrs T. is a 56-year-old woman who had a stroke about three months before the entry. She has a left hemiparesis and some memory problems. She lives alone but is supported by a carer and a large extended family. Mrs T. was unemployed before the stroke.

Tuesday 7 March
I had to be up early today and be ready by 8.30 to go to physio at the hospital. I was picked up early today 9.20. When we got to the hospital we were not going to get any physio as most of the OTs had phoned in sick. So I did a bit of knitting and one of the therapists took me upstairs to the bathroom and assessed me getting in and out of the bath with a seat. I did quite well so she was going to order me one. The taxi driver came in about 11 o'clock to see if I was ready so I got home about 11.15. Not a very productive day.

Extract 3

Mrs J. is a 34-year-old woman who had a stroke about three months before the entry. She has residual problems with balance, headaches

(Continued)

(Continued)

and fatigue. She lives with her husband and two children and was also in employment outside the house before the stroke.

4 April
Sunday – I have felt good today, my forehead doesn't feel so tight today and I haven't felt quite as tired as yesterday!

My left leg muscles are rather achy today and I now feel sure that although they are probably hurting because I am walking more, the sensitivity to the pain has been caused by the stroke, as only one leg feels achy and it is the leg that thinks warm water in the bath is cold!!

Although the weekends are more active with Pete and the kids home, it is nice feeling the normality of everyday life.

Extract 4

Mr H. is a 50-year-old man who had a stroke two months before the entry. He has aphasia, with severe expressive and receptive language problems. He lives with his wife and adult children. Mrs H. is recording the diary as Mr H. is unable to. He was active and employed before the stroke.

Monday 8 March
Hospital today for 20 mins speech therapy and 20 mins occupational therapy. Colours, dot to dot, shapes etc. Some easy, some hard for Mr H. to do, he cannot understand why he has to go, but quite happy to do tasks and amazed when he cannot do them. Phoned Social Services about benefits, not entitled to anything except Disabled Living Allowance when Mr H. has had stroke for three months. I work more than 16 hrs so get on with it. Stroke Association have rung and left message on answer phone, will hear from them later.

Mr H. is building Meccano quite well, reading drawing plans and finding right parts.

Extract 5

Mr N. is an 80-year-old man who had a stroke and who kept a progress record on his calendar while he was in hospital.

June
Sunday 3   Took 400 steps unaided.
Monday 4   20 times across? wash room floor.
Tuesday 5   30 times across wash room floor.
Wednesday 6   35 times across wash room floor.
Thursday 7   40 times across wash room floor.

Friday 8   Walked back from physio – two flights of stairs and long corridor.
Saturday 9 to Wednesday 13   Walking without aid.
Thursday 14   Cooking 11.15.
Friday 15   Walking without aid.
Tuesday 19   Home visit with physios.

Analysing the content

For this exercise you may wish to either create several copies of the relevant extracts and use coloured marker pens, or type the extracts into a word processing package. Having read and reread the text, consider the following issues:

1   Briefly summarise what has happened in each extract.
2   Identify key themes/categories in each extract.
3   Develop a list of themes and categories.
4   Reread each text and highlight each theme and category.
5   Cut-and-paste each category.
6   Read and summarise each category, thinking about the similarities and differences between the texts. For example, if one extract includes a positive evaluation and another a negative, is it possible to identify why?
7   Begin to group the categories into themes and repeat the exercise.
8   Write an overview and use data to illustrate.

Analysing the structure

Since the material presented above takes the form of extracts not of full texts and includes only limited information on the context, the analysis of the structure of the text will be restricted. However you may wish to consider the following issues:

1   How and why was the text created?
2   How do you think the version presented here differs from the original text and how is this likely to affect the structure?
3   How is the story told and how does this differ between the extracts?
4   How does the author present him or herself?
5   What aspects of the narrative contained in the text form the basis for its interpretation?
6   How has the text been used, who determines its meaning and are alternative interpretations possible?

6

Conclusion: Exploiting the Potential
of Research Diaries

Key aims
- To consider the main strengths and weaknesses of diary research.

Key objectives
- To examine the nature of diary research and identify underlying issues.
- To examine the advantages and limitations of diaries in social research.
- To examine the types of knowledge created by diary research.

Diaries: their strengths and weaknesses
as methods of data collection

Diaries are very flexible ways of accessing information about activities and thoughts and feelings. They can be used in a variety of designs. Researchers engaged in experiments will use a highly structured diary/recording system while researchers using unsolicited diaries can access information which has not been 'contaminated' by the research process.

While diaries can be used as the sole source of information, they can also be used in combination with other methods. In the Expenditure and Food Survey, household expenditure on major items is assessed through a household interview but all other expenditure is assessed through diaries kept by household members (Botting, 2003, p. 162). Diaries can thus be used to identify expenditure on new items which can then be included in the interviews, such as the expenditure on mobile phones in the 1990s. The data generated by diaries will often form an important part of an overall body of information. In political histories diaries may be particularly important when other sources are more restricted or have been controlled by censorship, for example in the late seventeenth century in England. In social histories diaries are an important source that can be considered alongside other documents of life such as letters and wills. Diaries can also be explicitly linked to other forms of data collection. In the diary-interview approach participants in the research keep an observation log or diary which is then used as the basis of follow-up interviews (Zimmerman and Weider, 1977).

Diaries have two major advantages over other methods: they facilitate access to hard-to-reach or hard-to-observe phenomena, and they help overcome memory problems. Groups may be hard to access for research for a variety of reasons. Perhaps the most obvious reason is that potential informants are no longer alive. In such circumstances unsolicited diaries along with other documents of life provide virtually the only means of accessing how such individuals behaved and perceived the world. MacFarlane (1970) would have found it virtually impossible to recreate the mental world of a seventeenth century Essex vicar without Ralph Josselin's diary. In contemporary societies, hard-to-reach groups are often those who are marginalised or socially excluded. Such groups tend to distrust mainstream society and its representatives, which for them may include researchers. Using methods such as interviews and observation involves a considerable investment of time and energy in building up access and trust, and relatively intrusive methods can either alter the behaviour which the researcher wishes to observe or compromise the researcher. For example Humphreys's (1970) ethnographic study of sex in public places created considerable practical and ethical problems. To observe such acts he acted as a watchqueen, a 'voyeur-lookout' for the men engaged in illicit sex in public toilets (1970, p. 28). Using diaries avoids these problems. Jones and his colleagues (2000) in Hong Kong used diaries not only to record the experiences of men who have sex with men but also to access related attitudes, feelings and beliefs.

Most social science methodologies access information at one point in time, and researchers wanting to access information about things that occurred some time before usually have to rely on participants' memories of such phenomena. Such recollections are notoriously inaccurate and diaries enable individuals to make records at the time, minimising retrospection bias. Coxon (1999) undertook a study comparing diaries and questionnaires: 86 gay men completed a month-long sexual diary and subsequently 74 completed a follow-up questionnaire for the same period. Coxon identified discrepancies, and concluded that while the overall pattern of activity in the two sources of data is similar, the sexual diaries were more likely to provide accurate data (1999, p. 230).

Diaries do have limitations: some are common to all diary research, others are evident in specific forms of diary research. The most obvious common limitations relate to cost and selection bias.

While good quality social research is labour and therefore resource intensive, diary research tends to be more expensive than other types of social research. There are costs in developing the diary and recording equipment and training the diarists, especially when diaries are used as part of experimental or survey research. Researchers using unsolicited diaries have the expense of locating and using relevant archives. Researchers using solicited diaries need to deliver and collect the diaries and support the diarists while they are completing their diaries. Finally there is the expense of analysing the diary data. This may be particularly expensive for researchers who have to create or transcribe text. Corti describes the costs and benefits of diaries in the following way:

> The diary method is generally more expensive than the personal interview, and personal placement and pick-up visits are more costly than postal administration. If the diary is unstructured, intensive editing and coding will push up the costs. However, these costs must be balanced against the superiority of the diary method in obtaining more accurate data, particularly where the recall method gives poor results. (2003, p. 73)

Diaries also involve a selection bias. Diary keeping is a demanding and skilled activity and there is a systematic bias in terms of the individuals who are willing and able to keep a diary. It is particularly evident in unsolicited diaries where there is a strong bias towards social elites even when, as in the nineteenth century, diary keeping was a relatively common social habit. Pollock (1983) analysed the 'representativeness' of the diaries which she used for her study of adult–child relations in Britain and the USA. Her sample was biased as the diarists were drawn from the literate section of society. Eleven per cent of the sample belonged to the 'top ranking members of the upper classes' (1983, p. 71). The largest occupation group were the clergy followed by individuals employed in the arts and sciences. In terms of religious affiliation the sample was biased to Nonconformist groups: Puritans (10%), Quakers (12%) and dissenting sects (16%). Only in Britain was there more substantial representation from mainstream religious groups such as Church of England or Roman Catholic (17%).

Specific types of diaries may have their own limitations. In experimental and survey research diaries are often used because it is too expensive or difficult for the researcher to observe and record the required information. The researcher is dependent on the diarist for accuracy of recording and in some circumstances there may be incentives for the diarist not to record accurate information. For example individuals who suffer from chronic illnesses such as asthma or back-pain may wish to appear more compliant with prescribed treatment than they actually are. Stone and his colleagues (2003) undertook a study of the ways in which adults with chronic back pain used diaries. They randomly assigned participants to an experimental group whose members were invited to make three pain entries in paper diaries at specified times on 21 consecutive days, and to a control group who used an electronic diary with visible date-stamped entries. They found that the 40 individuals who completed electronic diaries and were aware that the timing of their record was being recorded had a 94% compliance rate. In contrast the 40 individuals who completed paper diaries but were not aware that the timing of their record was in fact being recorded reported a compliance rate of 90%. However their actual compliance rate as recorded by the concealed electronic device was 11% (completion within the specified 30 minute window; an additional 9% completed within a broader 90 minute window). Such findings indicate that traditional paper-based diaries are not a reliable source of factual information, although electronic systems in which participants are aware that the timing of their entries is recorded do ensure greater compliance with instructions on when to complete entries.

Researchers using diaries as a mean of accessing information about social phenomena external to the diary need to be aware of a problem which is common to all documentary sources: the key role of the author or narrator in creating the text. Clarkson describes this in the following way:

> Documentary sources supply the empirical evidence that can support sociological theories. But documents are tricky; they tell us what the author wants us to know, which is not necessarily what the researcher is really interested in. They offer a version of events from the perspective of the narrator. This is the case even of documents generated officially, but the opportunities for putting a gloss on reality are all the greater in diaries, letters and memoirs. (2003, p. 82)

Comment

Diaries are flexible: they can form part of a variety of research designs, including experimental and survey designs, historical research and ethnographic or naturalistic research, and can be used in combination with other methods of data collection. They are particularly effective in accessing information which is difficult to access in other ways. However it is also important to note that diaries have limitations. They can be expensive to use and they may introduce a selection bias into the research. They need to be used with care.

Box 6.1 Diaries: advantages and limitations

Overall advantages

- Flexible, can be used in a range of designs
- Can take a variety of forms from highly structured to unsolicited
- Can be used in combination with other methods

Specific advantages

- Can be used to access hard-to-reach groups
- Can be used to record hard-to-observe behaviours
- Minimise memory problems

Limitations

- Cost
- Selection bias
- Possible inaccuracies and biases

Diaries: a natural or an artificial method of data collection?

In a number of ways diary research is 'natural', i.e. not imposed on or alien to individuals who participated in the research. In his discussion of the use of diaries in Project SIGMA, Coxon noted that 'the diary method grew out of our [the researchers'] experience as sexually active gay men' (1996, p. 20). It was more natural than alternatives such as interviewing because:

- It existed as common social practice prior to the research. Diary keeping seems to be common among gay men, and there are some famous examples of published diaries such as Joe Orton's (1986).
- It developed out of common social practice. Several of the researchers had kept sexual diaries for a number of years before the research and they drew on their own experience in developing the method.
- Diarists described their experiences in their own words: they used 'natural language' (1996, pp. 19–21).

While Project SIGMA used diaries as part of a survey of the sexual behaviour of gay men, the 'naturalness' of diaries makes them particularly attractive for researchers who wish to minimise the intrusiveness of the research process. However there are important limits to the 'naturalness' of diaries. Diary keeping is a learnt behaviour that only developed when certain conditions were met. These conditions include the:

- existence of a vernacular writing system
- development of an education system and a critical mass of literate individuals
- access to the necessary writing equipment
- motivation to keep a personal record including sufficient personal security to protect from exposure.

These conditions have been met occasionally in premodern societies: for example in tenth century Japan a literate leisured elite kept personal records. Since the seventeenth century the increasing literacy and the falling costs of writing have created the necessary conditions for more widespread diary keeping. In the early modern period, the sixteenth and seventeenth centuries, religion especially Puritanism provided a strong stimulus. In the later period there has been a wider range of stimuli, not least the personal and financial benefits of publication. However given the discipline and effort required to keep a regular record, diary keeping in contemporary societies remains a minority habit which tends to be more developed among literary elites.

Diary keeping is a sophisticated activity involving a set of social conventions and requiring access to specific resources. In comparison to some approaches to data collection such as semi-structured interviews, diary research can be considered a relatively artificial activity. Semi-structured interviews can be seen as a form of guided conversation and therefore the researcher can assume that the participant knows what is going on and can draw on their experience of previous everyday conversations. Indeed the researcher may strive to make the interview as like a normal conversation as possible to maximise the richness of the data produced by the interview. In contrast researchers using diaries cannot take for granted such tacit lay knowledge. Most participants in diary research will not have previous experience of diary keeping and therefore the researcher will need to explicitly explain the aims and objectives of the diary and provide guidance on the conventions of diary research. Indeed the extent to which diarists adhere to the conventions of diary keeping and the ways in which they breach them may be an interesting aspect of the study. In Meth's (2003) study of African women's experience of domestic violence, 18 of the 39 diaries included past events in the daily recording. Such events were not used to illustrate a contemporary event but there was 'the explicit structuring or writing of the diary around and on past events, even using "historical" dates as headings' (2003, p. 198).

Comment

Researchers using diaries need to be aware of the distinctive characteristics of diary keeping that will form the context of their study. While diary keeping is a recognisable form of social behaviour even in those groups where it is widespread, it is a minority habit. Researchers using unsolicited diaries will need to consider how far the diarists in their study were typical or unusual. Researchers soliciting diaries need to consider the tacit knowledge used by diarists and the ways in which the participants in their study can access such knowledge.

Box 6.2 Diaries: natural and artificial elements

Natural elements

- Established social practice
- Use diarists' own words
- Minimise intrusion, diarists can choose when and where to make entries

Artificial elements

- Depend on implicit conventions
- Require specific skills
- Need specific resources
- Need personal security

Fitness for the purposes of research

- Experimental/survey researchers use structured questionnaire-like diaries
- Historical/naturalistic researchers emphasise and exploit the naturalistic aspects of diaries

Diaries and knowledge

Researchers use methodologies to access knowledge. Such knowledge may be difficult to access for a number of reasons, for instance because the people who can supply it are difficult to access, or the events are rare or concealed, or the researcher is interested in how events are experienced. Berman in his discussion of ways of developing knowledge about ageing noted:

> Once we acknowledge that descriptions of age-related experiences are part of the knowledge of aging, the value of personal journals as a source of such descriptions becomes readily apparent. (1988, p. 61)

Such flexibility raises questions about the nature and status of the knowledge which is accessed and it is important that the researcher using diaries is aware of such debates and controversies.

Positivism

When the social sciences matured as academic disciplines in the nineteenth century, social scientists treated knowledge about society as the same as knowledge about the natural world. Durkheim, in his study of suicide, described the development of knowledge in the following way:

> A scientific investigation can thus be achieved only if it deals with comparable facts, and it is the more likely to succeed the more certainly it has combined all those that can be usefully compared ... the botanist, speaking of flowers or fruits, the zoologist of fish or insects, employ these terms in previously determined senses. (1952, pp. 41–2)

Durkheim argued that suicide rates were social facts and his role was to collect and organise these facts and then to use them to develop theories about society. In experimental and survey research, diaries are often treated as a straightforward record of facts and the main concern of the researcher is to ensure that this record is as accurate as possible. While positivism has been subject to major criticism in the social sciences, there can be no doubt that it continues to underpin much research especially in the natural sciences. Medical scientists use experiments to explore the ways in which various interventions affect human subjects. In this context diaries can generate a certain type of knowledge. Parkin and his colleagues (2000) used diaries and other methods of data collection to examine the effects of beta interferon treatment of multiple sclerosis. Survey research can also be used in the same way. For example in the 1990s the diary component of the Expenditure and Food Survey identified increasing expenditure on mobile phones indicating that they were becoming a regular element in most households' expenditure. In 1996–97 such expenditure was included as an item in the questionnaire component of the survey (King, 1997, p. 179). The survey was confirming what most individuals could observe for themselves, that mobile phone use had become an established habit and mode of communication in British society in the 1990s.

Social constructionism

While Durkheim in his study of the facts related to suicide was keen to differentiate between scientific definitions of facts and facts as embodied in 'ordinary terminology' or the 'words of common usage' (1952, p. 41), critics of his approach suggest that the positivist approach involves precisely this confounding. It fails to recognise the ways in which social facts, such as suicide, are socially constructed. Taylor (1982) in his analysis of suicide on the London Underground examined the ways in which the coroners' courts treated such deaths. He found that for a death to be classified as suicide, not only did the investigation of the circumstances indicate that the 'death looked like suicide' but the individual's history was reconstructed to form 'an appropriately suicidal biography' (1982, p. 121). When a death is classified as a suicide this is a social reality which has real consequences, but it is also a socially constructed reality, the 'product of an organisational process of knowledge production', and reflects 'officials' beliefs and ideas about suicide (as well as those of other interested parties)' (1982, p. 122). Such an approach implies the main focus of attention should be on the ways in which social reality is socially constructed.

This approach to knowledge is most clearly articulated in social constructionism, which starts from the premise that knowledge is not a static phenomenon – facts which individuals collect – but is actively created or constructed through the processes which individuals use to organise and make sense of everyday life. Schwandt describes this in the following way:

> Most of us would agree that knowing is not passive – a simple imprinting of sense data on the mind – but active; that is, mind does something with these impressions, at the very least forming abstractions or concepts. In this sense, constructivism means that human beings do not find or discover knowledge so much as we construct or make it. We invent concepts, models and schemes to make sense of experience, and we continually test and modify these constructions in the light of new experience. (2000, p. 197)

This approach draws attention to the conventions which underpin the process of making sense, especially the taken-for-granted and shared conventions which are central to individual and collective understanding and action.

Researchers who want to explore the ways in which such social conventions structure social reality require methodologies which can capture and analyse the relevant processes. Given the importance of actual social practices and the centrality of the ways in which individuals use language in its many forms, for example in conversations, stories, narrative or discourses, then the emphasis is on capturing and analysing language as it is used to identify the structures which underpin and shape such usage:

how utterances work is a matter of understanding social practices and analyzing the rhetorical strategies in play in particular kinds of discourse. (Schwandt, 2000, p. 197)

Diaries provide one way of accessing the natural usage of language. Both solicited and unsolicited diaries involve the creation of texts which make use of social conventions to make sense of and present what is happening to an individual. Such conventions can be identified through structural analysis. For example Jones and his colleagues (Jones et al., 2000; Jones and Candlin, 2003) in their study of men who have sex with other men used diaries to explore the conventions which diarists used to account for their actions. Similarly Crossley analysed the ways in which John Diamond (2001) used his diary, initially a weekly column in *The Times*, to make sense of and communicate his experience of living with and dying from oral cancer. Crossley treated Diamond's 'diary' as a text which Diamond constructed to make his experiences accessible.

Critical realism

Social constructionism explores the conventions that underpin interaction but does not necessarily exhaust the knowledge which may be contained in diaries. For example Taylor's (1982) study identified the ways in which social conventions underpin the official classification of some deaths as suicide, but as Taylor acknowledged (1982, p. 122) this does not alter the reality that people kill themselves. Similarly an analysis of the conventions of John Diamond's diary does not alter the fact that he died of oral cancer. Critical realism is an attempt to integrate these different aspects of reality, linking an awareness that one form of reality consists of 'human–made, socially produced ... "social constructs", abstract and cultural artefacts and institutions' (Ilkka, 2002, p. viii) with an awareness that some forms of reality exist independently of such constructs and that scientific theories attempt to access the truth about such realities. While they can never totally capture such reality, 'good scientific theories typically are false but nevertheless "close to the truth"' (2002, p. vi). Thus critical realism emphasises the importance of developing theories which capture true information about reality:

> a scientific realist sees theories as attempts to reveal the true nature of reality even beyond the limits of empirical observation. A theory should be *cognitively successful* in the sense that the theoretical entities it postulates really exist and the lawlike descriptions of these entities are true. Thus, the basic aim of science for a realist is *true information about reality*. The realist of course appreciates empirical success like the empiricist. But for the realist, the truth of a theory is a precondition for the adequacy of scientific explanations. (italics in the original: 2002, p. 167)

Such an approach enables the researcher to consider the data recorded in diaries as more than just a collection of facts or a social construct which provides insight into the underpinning social conventions: they are the raw material that can be used in the development of theory. While the process of diary production shapes such materials, diaries can be interrogated to examine what insight they provide on realities external to the diary. As Clarkson (2003, p. 82) has noted, diaries are documents and as such can be used for theorising if treated with care.

As long as diaries are systematically scrutinised and due account is taken of the contexts within which they are written, the data collected can be used as a valuable source for theorising about the social realities of the world in which the diarist lived. Of course much of anthropological theory about other cultures has been derived from theorising about the content of journals, i.e. fieldnotes, but only exceptionally has this process been made transparent as in Geertz's (1988) analysis of Malinowki's and Read's texts. Barley's (1986) account of his own fieldwork is a conscious attempt to make his theorising transparent by placing it within a personal biographical context.

While diary data can be used for theorising about various aspects of social reality, they are particularly important as a source of data for change over time. By using documentary sources covering 400 years, Pollock (1983, p. 199) was able to convincingly challenge the theory that over time parental treatment of their children had become less brutal and more equal.

Diary data can of course be used to theorise about contemporary social reality, and are perhaps particularly valuable in accessing intimate and highly personal issues related to areas such as sexuality or illness. The Project SIGMA diaries generated a very rich source of data on the sexual behaviour of men who have sex with men. Coxon (1996) used these data to reflect on the theories that had emerged to explain one key fact, the increase in risky sexual behaviour in the 1990s. He identified two major theories: the 'relapse theory', which postulated that a significant minority of gay men who adopted safe sex when the risks created by HIV infection first became evident reverted to unprotected sex; and the 'negotiated safety' theory, in which partners agreed on the level of risk they were willing to accept. He argued that both theories failed to reflect and explain the data captured in the Project SIGMA diaries. Both theories provided relatively standardised explanations of behaviours that in reality varied considerably according to context, and both overemphasised cognitive processes. He suggested that:

> often the '3D theory' comes closer to describing reality: 'It was dark, I was drunk and I didn't have a condom'. (1996, p. 172)

Comment

Diaries can be used in many different ways, and the types of knowledge they represent and can provide access to depends on how they are used. If the researcher operates within a positivistic tradition – and much of experimental research and survey research falls within that tradition – then little attention is paid to the nature of knowledge, as facts are seen as virtually self-evident and easy to identify. The emphasis is on the technology that will ensure minimal distortion and bias and maximise accuracy in fact collection. In contrast, researchers working within a social constructionist tradition see 'facts' as essentially problematic and are interested in getting below the surface, looking behind the screens to see how facts such as suicide rates are created. Researchers working within a critical realist tradition take an intermediate position. Like positivists they are interested in getting at the truth, but unlike positivists they do not see it as easy or even possible to get the whole truth; they recognise that theories only approximate. They are only truthlike and can always be improved and developed.

Box 6.3 Diaries and knowledge

	Positivist	Constructionist	Critical realist
Nature of knowledge	Facts	Social constructs	Fallible truthlike theories
Role of researcher	To gather and classify facts	To make explicit and visible the rules and conventions which underpin social constructs	To develop theories which are as truthlike as possible
Utility of diaries	Source of facts	Analysis provides insight into structuring of the text	Source of raw material for theorising

Final comment

Diaries are intrinsically fascinating documents that have a recognised role and value in contemporary society. Many of them can and should be read for pleasure. They are also an important resource for social and other researchers. While they have to be treated with respect, and they do not represent a cheap or necessarily easy to use method, they can either on their own or in combination with other methods generate a unique body of information.

References

Acton, C. (2003) Conversational analysis, in R.L. Miller and J.D. Brewer (eds) *The A–Z of Social Research*, Sage, London, pp. 48–53.

Alaszewski, A. and Alaszewski, H. (2005) Stroke and younger people: a longitudinal study of post-stroke normalisation and rehabilitation, http://www.kent.ac/chss/frames/index. dtm. accessed 20 September 2004.

Alaszewski, A., Alaszewski, H., Ayer, S. and Manthorpe, J. (2000) *Managing Risk in Community Practice: Nursing, Risk and Decision Making*, Balliere Tindall, Edinburgh.

Alaszewski, H., Alaszewski, A., Potter, J., Penhale, B. and Billings, J. (2003) Life after stroke: reconstructing everyday life, CHSS, University of Kent, Canterbury, http:// www.kent.ac.uk/chss/pages/docs/stroke.pdf.

Altschuler, E.L. (2001) One of the oldest cases of schizophrenia in Gogol's *Diary of a Madman, British Medical Journal*, December, 323, pp. 1475–7.

Anne Frank House (n.d.) *A Museum with a Story,* Anne Frank House, Amsterdam.

Arksey, L. (1983) *American Diaries: an Annotated Bibliography of Published American Diaries and Journals*, vol. 1, Gale Research, Detroit, MI.

Arksey, L. (1986) *American Diaries: an Annotated Bibliography of Published American Diaries and Journals*, vol. 2, Gale Research, Detroit, MI.

Armstrong, H. (2005) Unleashing the inner monologue, http://www.dooce.com, accessed 8 February 2005.

Atkinson, R. and Flint, J. (2003) Sampling, snowball: accessing hidden and hard-to-reach populations in R.L. Miller and J.D. Brewer (eds) *The A–Z of Social Research*, Sage, London, pp. 274–80.

Backsheider, P.R. (ed.) (1992) *Daniel Defoe: a Journal of the Plague Year,* Norton, New York.

Bain, J.D., Ballantyne, R., Packer, J. and Mills, C. (1999) Using journal writing to enhance student teachers' reflexivity during field experience placements, *Teachers and Teaching: Theory and Practice*, 5, pp. 51–73.

Bale, T. (1999) Dynamics of a non-decision: the 'failure' to devalue the pound, 1964–7, *Twentieth Century British History*, 10, pp. 192–217.

Barbellion, W.N.P. (1919) *Journal of a Disappointed Man*, Chatto and Windus, London.

Barley, N. (1986) *The Innocent Anthropologist: Notes from a Mud Hut*, Penguin, Harmondsworth.

Beaglehole, J.C. (1988a) *The Journals of Captain James Cook on his Voyages of Discovery: the Voyage of the Endeavour, 1768–1771, Part One*, Kraus Reprint, Millwood, NY.

Beaglehole, J.C. (1988b) *The Journals of Captain James Cook on his Voyages of Discovery: the Voyage of the Resolution and Discovery, 1776–1780, Part Four*, Kraus Reprint, Millwood, NY.

Beales, D. (1982) Gladstone and his diary: 'Myself, the worst of all interlocutors', *The Historical Journal*, 25, pp. 463–9.

Becker, H.S. (2002) The life history and the scientific mosaic, in D. Weinberg (ed.) *Qualitative Research Methods*, Blackwell, Oxford, pp. 79–87.

Bennett, A. (1998) *Writing Home*, Faber and Faber, London.

Berman, H.J. (1988) Admissible evidence: geropsychology and the personal journal, in S. Reinharz and G.D. Rowles (eds) *Qualitative Gerontology*, Springer, New York, pp. 47–63.

Biernacki, P. and Wald, W. (1981) Snowball sampling: Problems and techniques of chain referral sampling, *Sociological Methods and Research*, 10, pp 141–63.

Blaikie, N. (2000) *Designing Social Research*, Polity, Cambridge.

Bolger, N., Davis, A. and Rafaeli, P. (2003) Diary methods: capturing life as it is lived, *Annual Review of Psychology*, 54, pp. 579–616.

Botankie, E. (1999) Seventeenth-century Englishwomen's spiritual diaries: self-examination, covenanting, and account keeping, *Sixteenth Century Journal*, 30, pp. 3–21.

Botting, B. (2003) *Family Spending: a Report on the 2001–2002 Expenditure and Food Survey*, Stationery Office, London.

Boulton, J.T. (ed.) (1991) *Daniel Defoe: Memoirs of a Cavalier*, Oxford University Press, Oxford.

Bowling, A. (2002) *Research Methods in Health: Investigating Health and Health Services*, 2nd edn, Open University Press, Maidenhead.

Bowring, R. (1982) *Murasaki Shikubu: Her Diary and Poetic Memoir*, trans. and ed. R. Bowring, Princeton University Press, Princeton, NJ.

Brewer, J. (2003a) Positivism, in R.L. Miller and J.D. Brewer (eds) *The A–Z of Social Research*, Sage, London, pp. 235–7.

Brewer, J. (2003b) Content analysis, in R.L. Miller and J.D. Brewer (eds) *The A–Z of Social Research*, Sage, London, pp. 43–5.

Brewer, J. (2003c) Induction, in R.L. Miller and J.D. Brewer (eds) *The A–Z of Social Research*, Sage, London, pp. 154–6.

Brewer, J. (2003d) Deduction, in R.L. Miller and J.D. Brewer (eds) *The A–Z of Social Research*, Sage, London, pp. 67–9.

Brown, J. (2005) The drooling minutiae of childhood revealed for all to see as 'Mommy blogs' come of age, *The Independent*, 5 February, p. 7.

Bryman, A. (2001) *Social Research Methods*, Oxford University Press, Oxford.

Carter-Ruck, P.F., Skone James, E.P. and Skone James, F.E. (1965) *Copyright*, Faber and Faber, London.

Charmaz, K. (2000) Grounded theory: objectivist and constructivist methods, in N.K. Denzin and Y.S. Lincoln (eds) *Handbook of Qualitative Research*, Sage, London, pp. 509–35.

Charmaz, K. (2003) Grounded theory: objectivist and constructivist methods, in N.K. Denzin and Y.S. Lincoln (eds) *Strategies of Qualitative Inquiry*, Sage, Thousand Oaks, CA, pp. 249–91.

Clarkson, L. (2003) Documentary sources, in R.L. Miller and J.D. Brewer (eds) *The A–Z of Social Research*, Sage, London, pp. 80–3.

Cochrane, A.L. (1972) *Effectiveness and Efficiency: Random Reflections on Health Services*, The Nuffield Provincial Hospitals Trust, London.

Cooper, C. (2003) Analysis of variance (ANOVA), in R.L. Miller and J.D. Brewer (eds) *The A–Z of Social Research*, Sage, London, pp. 9–12.

Corti, L. (1993) Using diaries in social research, *Social Research Update*, issue 2, University of Surrey, Guildford, http://www.soc.surrey.ac.uk/sru/SRU2.html.

Corti, L. (2003) Diaries, self-completion, in R.L. Miller and J.D. Brewer (eds) *The A–Z of Social Research*, Sage, London, pp. 69–74.

Corti, L., Foster, J. and Thompson, P. (2003) Qualitative research data, archiving, in R.L. Miller and J.D. Brewer (eds) *The A–Z of Social Research*, Sage, London, pp. 241–6.

Coxon, A.P.M. (1982) *The Users' Guide to Multidimensional Scaling*, Heinemann, London.

Coxon, A.P.M. (1996) *Between the Sheets: Sexual Diaries and Gay Men's Sex in the Era of AIDS*, Cassell, London.

Coxon, A.P.M. (1999) Parallel accounts? Discrepancies between self-report (diary) and recall (questionnaire) measures of the same sexual behaviour, *Aids Care*, 11, pp. 221–34.

Coxon, A.P.M. and McManus, T.J. (2000) How many account for how much? Concentration of high-risk sexual behaviour among gay men, *Journal of Sex Research*, 37, pp. 1–7.

Craggs, A. (2003) *Family Spending: a Report on the 2002–2003 Expenditure and Food Survey*, The Stationery Office, London.

Crossley, M.L. (2003) 'Let me explain': narrative emplotment and one patient's experience of oral cancer, *Social Science and Medicine*, 56, pp. 439–48.

Crossman, R. (1977) *The Diaries of a Cabinet Minister. Volume Three, Secretary of State for Social Services 1968–70*, Hamilton and Cape, London.

Darwin, C. (1888) *A Naturalist's Voyage: Journal of Researches into the Natural History and Geology of the Countries Visited during the Voyage of H.M.S. 'Beagle' round the World*, Murray, London.

Darwin, C. (1951) *The Origin of Species by Means of Natural Selection or, the Preservation of Favoured Races in the Struggle for Life, a Reprint of the 6th Edition 1888*, Oxford University Press, Oxford.

de la Bédoyère (ed.) (1994) *The Diary of John Evelyn*, Headstart History, Bangor.

de Munck, V.C. (1998) Participant observation: a thick explanation of conflict in a Sri Lankan village, in V.C. de Munck and E.J. Sobo (eds) *Using Methods in the Field: a Practical Introduction and Casebook*, AltaMira, Walnut Creek, CA, pp. 39–54.

Denzin, N.K. and Lincoln, Y.S. (2000) Introduction: the discipline and practice of qualitative research, in N.K. Denzin and Y.S. Lincoln (eds) *Handbook of Qualitative Research*, Sage, London, pp. 1–28.

Diamond, J. (1999) *Because Cowards get Cancer Too*, Vermilion, London.

Diamond, J. (2001) *Snake Oil and Other Preoccupations*, Vintage, London.

Durkheim, E. (1952) *Suicide: a Study in Sociology*, Routledge and Kegan Paul, London.

Elliott, H. (1997) The use of diaries in sociological research on health experience, *Sociological Research Online*, 2 (2), http://www.socresonline.org.uk/socresonline/2/2/7.html, accessed 1 July 2004.

Emerson, R.M., Fretz, R.I. and Shaw, L.L. (1995) *Writing Ethnographic Fieldnotes*, University of Chicago Press, Chicago.

ESDA Qualidata (2005) About ESDA Qualidata, http://www.esds.ac.uk/qualidata/about/introduction.asp, accessed 28 February 2005.

Fetterman, D.M. (1998) *Ethnography: Step by Step*, 2nd edn, Sage, Thousand Oaks, CA.

Fielding, N. (1993) Ethnography, in N. Gilbert (ed.) *Researching Social Life*, Sage, London.

Firth, R. (1989) Introduction, in B. Malinowski *A Diary in the Strict Sense of the Word*, Athlone, London.

Fitzpatrick, R., Davey, C., Buxton, M.J. and Jones, D.R. (2001) Criteria for assessing patient based outcome measures for use in clinical trials, in A. Stevens, K. Abrams, J. Brazier, R. Fitzpatrick and R. Lilford (eds) *The Advanced Handbook of Methods in Evidence Based Healthcare*, Sage, London, pp. 181–94.

Foster, J. and Sheppard, J. (1995) *British Archives: a Guide to Archive Resources in the UK*, 3rd edn, Macmillan, London.

Fothergill, R.A. (1974) *Private Chronicles: a Study of English Diaries*, Oxford University Press, London.

Foucault, M. (1979) What is an author?, in J.V. Harari (ed.) *Textual Strategies*, Ithaca, NY, pp. 149–50.

Fox, R.C. (1957) Training for uncertainty, in R.K. Merton, G.G. Reader and P.L. Kendall (eds) *The Student-Physician: Introductory Studies in the Sociology of Medical Education*, Harvard University Press, Cambridge, MA, pp. 207–41.

Frank, A. (1997) *The Diary of a Young Girl: the Definitive Edition*, ed. Otto H. Frank and Mirjam Presler, trans. Susan Massotty, Penguin, London.

Frank, O. (1997a) Foreword, in *The Diary of a Young Girl: the Definitive Edition*, ed. Otto H. Frank and Mirjam Presler, trans. Susan Massotty, Penguin, London, pp. v–viii.

Frank, O. (1997b) Afterword, in *The Diary of a Young Girl: the Definitive Edition*, ed. Otto H. Frank and Mirjam Presler, trans. Susan Massotty, Penguin, London, pp. 337–9.

Franzoni, R. (2004) *From Words to Numbers: Narrative, Data, and Social Sciences*, Cambridge University Press, Cambridge.

Geertz, C. (1988) *Works and Lives: the Anthropologist as Author*, Polity, Cambridge.

Gladstone, W.E. (1896) Gladstone to Purcell, 14 January 1896, in D.C. Lathbury (ed.) *Correspondence on Church and Religion of William Ewart Gladstone*, vols 1 and 2, London, 1910.

Gogol, N. (1972) *Diary of a Madman and Other Stories*, trans. with intro. R. Wilks, Penguin, London.

Goris, J.-A. and Marlier, G. (1970) *Albrecht Dürer: Diary of his Journey to the Netherlands 1520–1521*, intro. J.-A. Goris and G. Marlier, Lund Humphries, London.

Grady, C. (n.d.) Payment of research participants, http://www.bioethics.nih.gov/research/humanres/payment.pdf, accessed 18 February 2005.

Grady, C. (2001) Money for research participation: does it jeopardize informed consent?, *American Journal of Bioethics*, 1, pp. 40–4.

Griffith, H. and Jordan, S. (1998) Thinking of the future and walking back to normal: an exploratory study of patients' experiences during recovery from lower limb fracture, *Journal of Advanced Nursing*, 28, pp. 1276–88.

Hammersley, M. and Atkinson, P. (1983) *Ethnography: Principles in Practice*, Tavistock, London.

Hammersley, M. and Atkinson, P. (1995) *Ethnography: Principles in Practice*, 2nd edn, Routledge, London.

Havlice, P.P. (1987) *And So to Bed: a Bibliography of Diaries Published in English*, Scarecrow, Metuchen, NJ.

Hockliffe, E. (ed.) (1908) *The Diary of Rev. Ralph Josselin, 1616–1683*, Cambridge Society, 3rd series, vol. xv.

Howell, E. (2002) *Gulliver's Travels* and *Robinson Crusoe* and the genre of travel writing, unpublished MA thesis, University of Leeds.

Huff, C.A. (1985) *British Women's Diaries: a Descriptive Bibliography of Selected Nineteenth-Century Women's Manuscript Diaries*, AMS Press, New York.

Humphreys, L. (1970) *Tearoom Trade: a Study of Homosexual Encounters in Public Places*, Duckworth, London.

Hunter Blair, P. (1977) *An Introduction to Anglo-Saxon England*, 2nd edn, Cambridge University Press, Cambridge.

Hyland, M.E., Kenyon, C.A, Allen, R. and Howarth, P. (1993) Diary keeping in asthma: comparison of written and electronic methods, *British Medical Journal*, 306, pp. 487–9.

Ilkka, N. (2002) *Critical Social Realism*, Oxford University Press, Oxford.

Janson, T. (2002) *Speak: a Short History of Languages*, Oxford University Press, Oxford.

Johns Hopkins Medicine (2004) Payment or remuneration to human participants, http://irb.jhmi.edu/Guidelines/Payment_Remuneration.html, accessed 18 February 2005.

Jones, H. (1994) Introduction: interpreting documents, in P. Catterall and H. Jones (eds) *Understanding Documents and Sources*, Heinemann, Oxford, pp. 5–9.

Jones, R.H. and Candlin, C.N. (2003) Constructing risk across timescales and trajectories: gay men's stories of sexual encounters, *Health, Risk and Society*, 5, pp. 199–213.

Jones, R.H., Kwan, Y.K. and Candlin, C.N. (2000) A preliminary investigation of HIV vulnerability and risk behavior among men who have sex with men in Hong Kong, City University of Hong Kong, Hong Kong, http://personal.cityu.edu.hk/~enrodney/Research/hiv_related_research.htm, accessed 29 July 2003 and 8 June 2004.

Jordan, W.K. (ed.) (1966) *The Chronicle and Political Papers of King Edward VI*, Allen and Unwin, London.

Jordanova, L. (2000) *History in Practice*, Arnold, London.

Kafka, F. (1976) *The Trial, America, The Castle, Metamorphosis, In the Penal Settlement, The Great Wall of China, Investigations of a Dog, Letter to his Father, The Diaries 1910–23*, Secker & Warburg/Octopus, London.

Kiernan, M. (ed.) (1985a) *Sir Francis Bacon, the Essayes or Counsels, Civill and Morall*, Clarendon, Oxford.

Kiernan, M. (ed.) (1985b) Introduction, in M. Kiernan (ed.) *Sir Francis Bacon, the Essayes or Counsels, Civill and Morall*, Clarendon, Oxford.

King, J. (1997) *Family Spending: a Report on the 1996–97 Family Expenditure Survey*, The Stationery Office.

Kitzinger, J. and Barbour, R.S. (eds) (1999) *Developing Focus Group Research: Politics, Theory and Practice*, Sage, London.

Kreuger, R. (1994) *Focus Groups: a Practical Guide for Applied Research*, 2nd edn, Sage, London.

Latham, R. (ed.) (1985) *The Shorter Pepys*, selected and ed. R. Latham, Bell and Hyman, London.

Latham, R. and Matthews, W. (eds) (1970a) The diary as history, in *The Diary of Samuel Pepys, Volume I, 1660*, Bells, London, pp. lxviii–xcvi.

Latham, R. and Matthews, W. (eds) (1970b) Previous editions, in *The Diary of Samuel Pepys, Volume I, 1660*, Bells, London, pp. lxviii–xcvi.

Lilford, R.J. and Stevens, A. (2001) Introduction: clinical trials, in A. Stevens, K. Abrams, J. Brazier, R. Fitzpatrick and R. Lilford (eds) *The Advanced Handbook of Methods in Evidence Based Healthcare*, Sage, London, pp. 7–9.

MacArthur, E. (2005) Audio and video clips, http://www.teamellen.com/ellen-article-1017.html, accessed 28 January 2005.

MacFarlane, A. (1970) *The Family Life of Ralph Josselin: a Seventeenth-Century Clergyman. An Essay in Historical Anthropology*, Cambridge University Press, Cambridge.

McClellan, J. (2005) Just do it ... blog it, The *Guardian,* Thursday 5 May 2005, http://www.guardian.co.uk/online/story/0,,1476175,00 html, accessed 31 May 2005.

McColl, E., Jacoby, A., Thomas, L., Soutter, J., Bamford, C., Steen, N., Thomas, R., Harvey, E., Garratt, A. and Bond, J. (2001) The conduct and design of questionnaire surveys in healthcare research, in A. Stevens, K. Abrams, J. Brazier, R. Fitzpatrick and R. Lilford (eds) *The Advanced Handbook of Methods in Evidence Based Healthcare*, Sage, London, pp. 247–71.

McCrum, R. (1998) *My Year Off: Rediscovering Life after a Stroke*, Picador, London.

Malinowski, B. (1966) *Coral Gardens and Their Magic*, Allen and Unwin, London.

Malinowski, B. (1989) *A Diary in the Strict Sense of the Word*, Athlone, London.

Marsh, C. (1982) *The Survey Method: the Contribution of Surveys to Sociological Explanation*, Allen and Unwin, London.

Matthews, W. (1945) *American Diaries*, University of California Press, Berkeley, CA.

Matthews, W. (1950) *British Diaries: an Annotated Bibliography of British Diaries Written between 1442 and 1942*, University of California Press, Berkeley, CA.

Merton, R.K. (1957) Some preliminaries to a sociology of medical education, in R.K. Merton, G.G. Reader and P.L. Kendall (eds) *The Student-Physician: Introductory Studies in the Sociology of Medical Education*, Harvard University Press, Cambridge, MA, pp. 3–79.

Merton, R.K., Reader, G.G. and Kendall, P.L. (eds) (1957) *The Student-Physician: Introductory Studies in the Sociology of Medical Education*, Harvard University Press, Cambridge, MA.

Meth, P. (2003) Entries and omissions: using solicited diaries in geographic research, *Area*, 35 (2), pp. 195–205.

Miller, K.A. (1985) *Emigrants and Exiles: Ireland and the Irish Exodus to North America*, Oxford University Press, New York.

Miller, R. (2003a) Sampling, probability, in R.L. Miller and J.D. Brewer (eds) *The A–Z of Social Research*, Sage, London, pp. 268–73.

Miller, R. (2003b) Statistical interaction, in R.L. Miller and J.D. Brewer (eds) *The A–Z of Social Research*, Sage, London, pp. 306–8.

Morgan, J. (1977) Editor's note, in R. Crossman, *The Diaries of a Cabinet Minister. Volume Three, Secretary of State for Social Services 1968–70*, Hamilton and Cape, London, pp. 9–12.

Morley, J. (1903) *The Life of William Ewart Gladstone*, vols 1–3, Macmillan, New York.

Morris, I. (ed.) (1970) *The Pillow Book of Sei Shonagon*, trans. and ed. Ivan Morris, Penguin, Harmondsworth.

Moser, C.A. and Kalton, G. (1971) *Survey Methods in Social Investigation*, 2nd edn, Heinemann, London.

Motion, A. (1993) *Philip Larkin: a Writer's Life*, Faber and Faber, London.

Muhr, T. (1997) *ATLAS/ti: User's Manual and Reference*, Scientific Software Development, Berlin.

Olivier Bell, A. (ed.) (1984) *The Diary of Virginia Woolf. Volume 5, 1936–41*, ed. Anne Olivier Bell, assisted Andrew McNeillie, Penguin, London.

Orton, J. (1986) *The Orton Diaries*, ed. J. Lahr, Methuen, London.

Papadopoulous, I. and Scanlon, K. (2002) The use of audio diaries with visually impaired people, *Journal of Visual Impairment and Blindness*, 96, pp. 456–59.

Parkin, D., McNamee, P., Jacoby, A., Miller, P., Thomas, S. and Bates, D. (2000) Treatment of multiple sclerosis with interferon beta: an assessment of cost-effectiveness and quality of life, *Journal of Neurology, Neurosurgery and Psychiatry*, 68, pp. 144–9.

Parkin, D., Rice, N., Jacoby, A. and Doughty, J. (2004) Use of a visual analogue scale in a daily patient diary: modelling cross-sectional time-series data on health-related quality of life, *Social Science and Medicine*, 59, pp. 351–60.

Penn Library (2004) Finding diaries: research guide, http://gethelp.library.upenn.edu/guides/general/diaries.html, accessed 14 June 2004.

Pimlott, B. (2002) Dear diary …, *The Guardian, G2*, 18 October, pp. 2–3.

Plummer, K. (1983) *Documents of Life: an Introduction to the Problems and Literature of a Humanistic Method*, Allen and Unwin, London.

Plummer, K. (2001) *Documents of Life 2: an Invitation to Critical Humanism*, Sage, London.

Pollock, L.A. (1983) *Forgotten Children: Parent–Child Relations from 1500 to 1900*, Cambridge University Press, Cambridge.

Pool, B. (1974) Sir William Coventry, 1628–86; Pepys's mentor, *History Today*, 24 (2), pp. 104–11.

Porter, S. (2000) Qualitative research, in D.F.S. Cormack (ed.) *The Research Process in Nursing*, 4th edn, Blackwell Science, Oxford, pp. 141–52.

Postan, M.M. (1971) *Fact and Relevance: Essays on Historical Methods*, Cambridge University Press, Cambridge.

Project SIGMA (2003) *Gay Men's Sexual Diaries: Information about Sexual Diaries*, http://www.sigmadiaries.com, accessed 29 July 2003.

Raftery, J., Stevens, A. and Roderick, P. (2001) The potential use of routine datasets in health technology assessment, in A. Stevens, K. Abrams, J. Brazier, R. Fitzpatrick and R. Lilford (eds) *The Advanced Handbook of Methods in Evidence Based Healthcare*, Sage, London, pp. 136–48.

Read, K.E. (1965) *The High Valley*, Scribner, New York.

Redgrave, L. and Clark, A. (2004) Pulling through, *The Guardian Weekend*, 18 September, pp. 15–20.

Redlich, F. (1975) Autobiographies as sources for social history: a research program, *Vierteljahrschrift fur Sozial- und Wirtschaftsgeschichte*, 6, pp. 380–90.

Riessman, C.K. (1993) *Narrative Analysis*, Sage, Newbury Park, CA.

Riley-Doucet, C. and Wilson, S. (1997) A three-step method of self-reflection using reflective journal writing, *Journal of Advanced Nursing*, 25, pp. 964–8.

Roberts, B. (2002) *Biographical Research*, Open University Press, Buckingham.

Robinson, D. (1971) *The Process of Becoming Ill*, Routledge and Kegan Paul, London.

Ross, S., Counsell, C.E., Gillespie, W.J., Grant, A.M., Prescott, R.J., Russell, I.T., Colthart, I.R., Kiauka, S., Russell, D. and Shepherd, S.M. (2001) Factors that limit the number, progress and quality of randomised controlled trials: a systematic review, in A. Stevens, K. Abrams, J. Brazier, R. Fitzpatrick and R. Lilford (eds) *The Advanced Handbook of Methods in Evidence Based Healthcare*, Sage, London, pp. 38–55.

Sahlins, M. (1995) *How 'Natives' Think: about Captain Cook, for Example*, University of Chicago Press, Chicago, IL.

Schutz, A. (1971) *Collected Papers. Vol. 1, The Problems of Social Reality*, Nijhoff, The Hague.

Schwandt, T.A. (2000) Three epistemological stances for qualitative inquiry: interpretivism, hermeneutics, and social constructionism, in N.K. Denzin and Y.S. Lincoln (eds) *Handbook of Qualitative Research*, Sage, London, pp. 189–213.

Seldon, A. (1994) Introduction: interpreting documents, in P. Catterall and H. Jones (eds) *Understanding Documents and Sources*, Heinemann, Oxford, pp. 29–31.

Sheridan, D. (ed.) (1991) *The Mass-Observation Diaries: an Introduction*, The Mass-Observation Archive (the University of Sussex Library) and the Centre for Continuing Education, University of Sussex, Falmer, http://www.sussex.ac.uk/library/massobs/diary_booklet.html, accessed 12 July 2004.

Shinagel, M. (ed.) (1994) *Daniel Defoe: Robinson Crusoe*, 2nd edn, Norton, New York.

Silverman, D. (1994) Analysing naturally-occurring data on AIDS counselling: some methodological and practical issues, in M. Boulton (ed.) *Challenge and Innovation: Methodological Advances in Social Research on HIV/AIDS*, Taylor and Francis, London.

Sissons Joshi, M., Senior, V. and Smith, G.P. (2001) A diary study of the risk perceptions of road users, *Health, Risk and Society*, 3, pp. 261–79.

Stake, R.E. (2003) Case studies, in N.K. Denzin and Y.S. Lincoln (eds) *Strategies of Qualitative Inquiry*, Sage, Thousand Oaks, CA, pp. 134–64.

Stewart, D. and Shamdasani, P. (1990) *Focus Groups: Theory and Practice*, Sage, London.

Stone, A.A., Shiffman, S., Schwartz, J.E., Broderick, J.E. and Hufford, M.R. (2003) Patient compliance with paper and electronic diaries, *Controlled Clinical Trials*, 24, pp. 182–99.

Strauss, A. and Corbin, J. (1990) *The Basics of Qualitative Research: Grounded Theory Procedures and Techniques*, Sage, London.

Stuhlmann, G. (ed.) (1974) *The Journals of Anaïs Nin 1934–1939*, Quartet, London.

Swanton, M. (2000) *The Anglo-Saxon Chronicles*, Phoenix, London.

Taylor, S. (1982) *Durkheim and the Study of Suicide*, Macmillan, London.

Thomas, W.I. and Znaniecki, F. (1958a) *The Polish Peasant in Europe and America*, vol. 1, Dover, New York.

Thomas, W.I. and Znaniecki, F. (1958b) *The Polish Peasant in Europe and America*, vol. 2, Dover, New York.

Thompson, P.R. (1988) *The Voice of the Past: Oral History*, 2nd edn, Oxford University Press, Oxford.

Tomalin, C. (2002) *Samuel Pepys: the Unequal Self*, Penguin, London.

Tosh, J. (1984) *The Pursuit of History: Aims, Methods and New Directions in the Study of Modern History*, Longman, London.

Uberoi, J.P.S. (1971) *Politics of the Kula Ring: an Analysis of the Findings of Bronislaw Malinowski*, 2nd edn, Manchester University Press, Manchester.

Weber, M. (1976) *The Protestant Ethic and the Spirit of Capitalism*, trans. Talcott Parsons, Allen and Unwin, London.

Wellard, S.J. and Bethune, E. (1996) Reflective journal writing in nurse education: whose interest does it serve?, *Journal of Advanced Nursing*, 24, pp. 1077–82.

Westhauser, K.E. (1994) Friendship and family in early modern England: the sociability of Adam Eyre and Samuel Pepys, *Journal of Social History*, 27, pp. 517–36.

Williams, M. (2002) Generalization in interpretive research, in T. May (ed.) *Qualitative Research in Action*, Sage, London, pp. 125–43.

WW2 People's War Team (2004) *About WW2 People's War*, http://www.bbc.co.uk/dna/ww2/About, accessed 15 June 2004.

Yushun, S. (2003) Party faithful, *The Guardian*, G2, 28 July, pp. 6–7.

Zimmerman, D.H. and Wieder, D.L. (1977) The diary-interview method, *Urban Life*, 5, pp. 479–98.

Index